Most people think that crossing the line means committing a crime, but it's not that simple. Sometimes the line you cross can be very blurred. For me, crossing the line is the gap between being honest with yourself and taking responsibility for your actions, and the other side, when things don't seem real anymore and you don't think about the consequences of what you're doing.

When you cross the line, everything seems to be happening too fast. Nothing seems rational and the people you respect, like your parents, don't seem to be making much sense. It is as if their voices are coming from a long way away, as if through water. You've switched off. The barriers have come down and all you can hear is the roaring in your ears.

For me, the roaring began when I was thirteen, but there had been problems long before that.

Carol Drinkwater is a successful actress and novelist, as well as an active campaigner and regular prison visitor. She has appeared in films such as *A Clockwork Orange* and numerous television series, including *All Creatures Great and Small*, where she played Helen Herriot. She is the author of four novels; *An Abundance of Rain*, *Akin to Love*, *Mapping the Heart* and *The Olive Farm*. In addition she has written three teenage novels: *The Haunted School*; *Molly* and *Molly on the Run* (which accompany a thirteen-part television series); and is working on two further novels. She divides her time between London and France.

Crossing the Line

Young Women and the Law

Carol Drinkwater, editor

Livewire
from The Women's Press

First published by Livewire Books, The Women's Press Ltd, 2000
A member of the Namara Group
34 Great Sutton Street, London EC1V 0LQ

British Library Cataloguing-in-Publication Data
A catalogue record for this book is available from the British Library.

ISBN 0 7043 4966 3

Typeset in 12/14pt Bembo by FSH Ltd, London
Printed and bound in Great Britain by Cox & Wyman,
Reading, Berkshire

Contents

Acknowledgements

I want to thank profoundly the young women who are here in print as well as those whose testimonies I have not used; all of them have trusted me and made these pages possible. The young women whose stories you are about to read have been given fictitious names, to protect them. Even shielded by anonymity, their trust and sharing have been acts of immense courage.

Aside from the girls, I would like to give very special thanks to Sister Kathleen Diamond for her faith, vision and practicality, and to Doctor Patrick de Mare who, during one of our treasured afternoons together, pointed out to me that the Greek word for *sin* is the same as for *not focusing*.

My heartfelt thanks also to Kirsty Dunseath, my splendid editor at The Women's Press; as well as her predecessor, Helen Windrath, who contracted the book from me; to Otto and Jill Wolff who have fed me and patiently talked through various stages of the book's development with me; to my husband, Michel Noll, for his feedback on the project; and to my very dear friend, Christopher Brown. Thanks also, to Steph Dardis in Kentish Town and to Reverend James McCarthy who is doing such splendid work with his shelter, THOMAS, for the homeless and marginalised in Blackburn and with his magazine, *Edges*. And lastly, to Amnesty International whose passion and tenacity have built an international voice synonomous with justice and integrity.

I have been astounded and humbled to discover how many people are out there working for minimal pay, if any, doing such sterling work, quietly making a significant difference in areas of society where it is much needed. The book is dedicated to you all.

Introduction

This book is not mine in the way that other writings have come from me. This collection belongs to the young women whose voices are on every page. I want to thank each one of them for the confidence they have entrusted in me, and for allowing me to share their stories.

What struck me most was the diversity of the women I met. Put together as a mosaic, their various experiences have led me to ask myself some fundamental questions about the law and what it means to 'cross the line'.

Technically, of course, crossing the line means breaking the law. The law is the rules of the game according to society. In order that society operates in a way that works for everyone we need a moral and social code that is clearly laid out and that we all understand and are expected to adhere to. When someone goes outside or beyond that structure, they are crossing the line. But what the contributors' experiences show is that it is not always so easy to decide who is the criminal and who is the victim. As one contributor says, 'There's always a reason why people do what they do.'

Of course, it is also impossible to know if someone who says they are innocent of a crime really is or not and I leave it to you, the reader, to make up your own mind. The point of this book is not to decide who is guilty and who is innocent; it is to show a few of the avenues that can lead someone into trouble in the first place and to shed light on what it is really like to become entangled in the legal system.

Most of the young women writing here have been through terrible experiences and one thing that you will notice as you read these stories is just how many of their lives have been touched by drugs. My eyes have been forced wide open to the dangerous role that the trafficking and consumption of drugs, particularly class A drugs, plays in our society today. I certainly had not grasped the extent to which drugs have a hold on the criminal environment, nor their far-reaching effects.

As so many of the contributors point out, drugs are a downward spiral ending in prison sentences and lifelong addictions. So why does anyone take that first shot of heroin, that first snort of cocaine?

Through drug use, many people are looking for fast solutions to difficult problems. Some seek oblivion because the ordeals and confusions they face are too tough to battle alone. Others see the sale of drugs as a quick cash return to help resolve personal or family crises. A lot of young women get into drugs because of boyfriends or pals. Whatever the reason, it is not long before they become hooked and are forced to steal or prostitute themselves to feed their habit.

The drug industry, second only to the armament industry, is one of the two most profitable industries in the world. The real traffickers, the drug barons, are not even lightly scarred by the imprisonment of young people who have been caught stealing, or the thousands of young women who are being used as mules. A mule is a person who carries an illegal item from one place to another for someone else's gain. The mule usually earns a modest sum for this service, or, perhaps, an air ticket to a dreamt-of location such as England. For the most part, mules tend to come from one of the Caribbean islands or from a South American country; areas that are known to produce a large amount of drugs. But the payment mules receive does not even begin to equal the risk they are taking. Importation, after murder and treason, carries some of the highest prison sentences within the British justice system. I wonder how many people are aware that simply saying yes to carrying some drugs can lead to up to fifteen years in prison.

Nevertheless, thousands of young women are being enticed by false promises of money if they will agree to transport drugs across frontiers, through customs or into prisons. These young women – and a small percentage of them are tricked and genuinely do not know they are carrying drugs – end up with very hefty prison sentences. What is little known is that, in a majority of cases, the identities of these women have been leaked to customs before their arrival by the very people who

3

employed them in the first place. Why would anyone want to do that? The answer is simple. On the same flight there will be one or two other people, usually business-men with suits and briefcases, smuggling in far greater quantities of the same drug. In order to pass through customs without being spotted they need a decoy, a dispensable cog in the powerful machine of international drug trafficking. In cases like this, how can we decide who the criminal really is?

Time and time again, the contributors tell stories of abuse and neglect, violence and betrayal. Is the most efficient way of helping these women and protecting society really to give them a criminal record or lock them away in prisons where their chances of freeing themselves from the past are often lessened, not increased?

This book is not intended as a judgement on the British prison system. Of course, they are overcrowded and drug infested, but I have also been deeply impressed by several extraordinary people who are working there with great integrity and compassion. What interests me is the system of justice itself: who should be condemned and why. Is prison the best place to send someone who has got into trouble, when prison is full of more experienced criminals who can share their 'knowledge'? Surely a system that obliges offenders to work within a community creates a better kind of social awareness as well as the opportunity to learn more positive skills? A few young people need to be held in a secured environment, but is prison really the best place? And wouldn't some of the money spent on prosecution and prisons be better spent on setting up drug rehabilitation centres and work-training schemes?

What I most hope for this book is that it proves to be a witness to its time and that it gives a voice to those who are frequently judged, but rarely understood.

What is clear from the stories in this book is that so many of the essentials in life have been missing for these women – love, compassion, stability and a secure environment. It is little wonder that so many look for the fundamentals elsewhere. If you find that any of the situations described in this book echo your own, there is a resource list at the end of this book, which will give you details about organisations that will be able to help.

Even if you are fortunate enough to have a stable home, loving friends and financial security, I hope this book will give you pause for reflection. We have so much work that needs to be done within our society and YOU are the future. You hold within your hands the possibility to make a difference, to change the world for the better. In order to do that, it is important to know what is going on around you. It's your world and your future. I hope that the words of these young women will inspire you, as they have me.

In order to protect the contributors' identities some names and places have been changed.

Carol

I'd never been in trouble with the police before but they got involved when I ran away from home. I was thirteen and extremely depressed. I had a problem – something it's still not easy for me to talk about. I didn't understand what was going on with me but I'd been feeling unhappy inside for more than six months. I couldn't talk to anyone about the confusion and all the mixed-up feelings and I think that's what led me into trouble – I'd reached crisis point.

The day I ran away, I got up in the morning feeling really low. We'd recently moved to a bigger house and I had an attic room right at the top. I came down the stairs in my school clothes as normal and said goodbye to my mum. But then I went down to our basement and changed out of my school uniform. I always intended to go home, I just didn't know when. I wanted people to take notice of me and I thought that, if I ran away, then everyone would ask me why and I would have to open up about what I was going through.

I didn't go too far – I just jumped on to a train and went to north London. At the time, I used to get about £5 a week dinner money and I had saved all of it for about five weeks. I got a cappuccino from Burger King and headed for a nearby park. The whole day was spent sitting on a bench, thinking about the different things that had been going on in my life and what was going to happen when I got home.

One of the big problems I had was that I never really got on with my dad. He's eight or nine years younger than my mum and she's Columbian. My parents didn't fight in front of me – I never saw them arguing or anything – but there were all these whispered conversations and there was always a lot of tension at home. What I didn't know then, and I know now, was that my father was having an affair with a woman at work. It made him aggressive but, because he was coming home so late, I'd assumed he was just having trouble at work. My school work started to slip because of my depression and that got me into even more trouble, which only made my problem worse.

I guess that, because my mum was pregnant with me when my parents got married, I felt as if it was somehow all my fault. But there were a lot of other things, too. I wasn't ready to speak about them at that stage, but I did manage to confide in one of my teachers. She made it easy for me to open up. Maybe it was because she was a lot younger than my mum, but old enough to know what I was talking about. But then this teacher, the only person I could talk to, left the school. She didn't abandon me or anything like that and she used to come and see me, but it wasn't the same. It was a loss and I couldn't deal with it.

The thing is that my major problem, my 'secret', was bulimia. I was bulimic and my bulimia and depression had a lot to do with loss, although at the time I was too confused to realise it. So, when this teacher left, it really hit me.

The first time I experienced loss was when I was nine. My best friend had cancer and he passed away just before he turned ten. It was a huge shock but I blocked it all out. Then, when I was twelve, my uncle died. I'd got on well with him and I really missed him. It was shortly after this that we moved to the bigger house. I had been sharing a room with my sister and had no privacy, but now I had the attic room and could do my own thing: throwing up. I was only eating one meal a day and then being sick and I don't really understand what made me do it. I don't know if I was trying to lose weight but, when I ate, I felt as if I had to get it out of me as quickly as possible and, when I did, it was a huge relief.

My teacher had put me in contact with the school counsellor when she left and she kept saying to me, 'You have to tell your parents, you can't live like this.' But I couldn't just spit it out like that. Then the counsellor started saying she would tell my parents herself and I knew I had to do something. I thought that if I ran away they'd ask me what it was all about and then I'd be forced to tell them.

So I just sat on that park bench wondering what I should do next. At one point this guy came and sat down beside me. He was really posh. He had this really expensive outfit on and, before he sat down, he got his handkerchief out and started wiping down the bench! I thought, 'Are you a snob or what?' He said, 'Oh, sorry, am I disturbing you?' and after that we started talking about lots of different things. He was Italian and had moved to England when he got divorced from his wife. I didn't want to tell him about my problems so I just said that there was a teachers' training thing on and that was why I was not at school. He asked me how old I was – he thought I looked between fifteen and eighteen, not thirteen. As I wasn't dressed up I was quite flattered that he thought I looked older.

He told me he never bought anything cheap and had pens in his pocket worth over £150. Somehow the conversation got on to the subject of presents and he asked me what sort of jewellery I liked. He said, 'Next time I bump into you I'll have a silver necklace inside my coat pocket for you.'

At the time I was really pleased to be having this great conversation with a complete stranger, although I did think it was weird the way he talked about us meeting again on the off-chance. Today, looking back on it, I realise it was risky and maybe now I'd be a bit more wary of talking to someone like that for so long. I guess I was lucky – he could have been anyone. We talked for about an hour and then he left.

I started walking around the park. It was getting dark and I realised I couldn't get home even if I wanted to. It got later and later, like one o'clock in the morning, and there I was, on a river bank, not planning to move. But I wasn't scared – although I was alone, I was happy to be away from everything. It was actually quite nice. But then I saw the police car.

By this time it was about four in the morning and this car kept driving around, passing me several times. I thought I would move so that the police couldn't see me but it was as if they were following me. They turned off down a main road so I decided to head back to where I had been sitting, but suddenly they zoomed up out of nowhere. They stopped me and asked me how old I was. I realised there was no point in lying. If I didn't tell them the truth they'd think I'd been up to all sorts of things, so I told them whatever they wanted to know. I had to get in the car with them and on the journey they kept asking all this stupid stuff, like, 'Have you got an abusive father?' and other things like that. I shouted back at them, 'No, no.'

They took me to the local police station, where I was lead into an office and told to sit down. It wasn't an interrogation room or anything like that and it was all quite casual. There were two other police officers as well as the bloke and woman who had picked me up. The woman was quite young, about twenty-five, and I ended up telling her I had an eating disorder. She told me that one of her friends had had a similar problem.

All the time they spoke to me, I just kept thinking, 'I'm not in the mood to hear all of this. I mean, it's not going to help me, is it?' I think I was incredibly rude to them because they were all so patronising and I was feeling very angry. They'd done their job – they'd brought me off the streets – and I didn't think they needed to keep on asking me all these stupid questions. It was as if they thought I couldn't be talked to in a mature way. 'Are you sure you've given us the right address? Are you sure you've given us the right telephone number?' YES!

The police phoned my parents and then drove me home. On the journey the policeman and woman tried to make conversation with me but I didn't want to talk. I was feeling nervous about what was going to happen next.

When I got home, my dad was standing at the door and he gave me a big hug. I was really sorry for what I'd done, causing them all that worry, and I think I started to cry. But I wasn't crying because I was glad to see them again – I think it was because I was incredibly scared of having to tell my parents the truth and I began to wish I'd just carried on as normal and kept my problem to myself.

In one of my earlier counselling sessions, the counsellor had asked me, 'If you tell your parents, what is the worst thing that could happen?' I answered, 'Things could get worse at home.' And that is exactly what happened. My dad hardly ever spoke to me again and he left home very soon after. I'd thought that my running away would bring me closer to him, but it didn't really make a difference. Also, because I had run away, the teacher I had confided in said she would only be able to write to me instead of seeing me. She's moved to South Africa now and I was upset at losing contact with her.

But people come and go. That's what I've found out. My uncle, my dad, the teacher – they go because they have to and I've learnt to deal with it. Recently one of my friends' mother died of cancer and my friend didn't come back to school for the rest of the year but, when she did, she seemed more mature. I think we are all more mature now. In the end it was a relief that my father left, although I do miss him at times. When I see him now we only talk about superficial things, stupid little conversations, but we are very similar – the same star sign, even.

I've also stopped blaming myself for everything that happened. I remember it clearly. I was in the car with Mum and she kept saying things like, 'You should take more responsibility, you should learn to control yourself.' I thought, 'No, wait a minute. This isn't all my fault. One, I didn't make Dad have an affair. Two, it wasn't me who made you pregnant. You are the one who should be taking more responsibility. All of this mess has nothing to do with me!' That's how I got through it all, I think. Things became a lot clearer.

Now I'm beginning to understand myself more. I'm learning Spanish because that is part of who I am. I feel as if I'm a bit of everything really – part Columbian, part

English, with some Irish and Welsh blood, too – but I like being part of such a mixed family. And, like almost everyone, I have a problem with my body image and complain about my hands, my feet, anything! But I'm finally beginning to accept myself. Learning to like myself at last.

Tara

Most people think that crossing the line means committing a crime, but it's not that simple. Sometimes the line you cross can be very blurred. For me, crossing the line is the gap between being honest with yourself and taking responsibility for your actions, and the other side, when things don't seem real anymore and you don't think about the consequences of what you're doing. It's like a storm in your ears.

When you cross the line, everything seems to be happening too fast. Nothing seems rational and the people you respect, like your parents, don't seem to be making much sense. It is as if their voices are coming from a long way away, as if through water. You've switched off. The barriers have come down and all you can hear is the roaring in your ears.

For me, the roaring began when I was thirteen, but there had been problems long before that. When I was about eight, nine or ten, maybe, my teacher at primary school used to abuse everyone in the class, including me and my sister, who was two years younger. (She has a drug problem now. We've all had problems.) It was a tiny school with only around twenty pupils and, every lunchtime, this teacher would let the boys go out first and then all the girls would rush out because the last ones would be caught by him and tickled and stuff. Also, he'd pick out three or four girls and do really graphic sex education. I was one of them.

The awful thing was, we'd tried to tell our parents but they didn't do anything about it. I remember saying to my mum, 'Our teacher does sex education classes and he *really* does it,' but she just said to me, 'Don't be silly.' I think she blanked it out. I've read that this is what a lot of mothers of abused children do – they sort of freeze because they can't bear the fact that something horrendous has happened to the child they love.

But, a couple of years later after I'd left that school and my sister was still there, some friends of my parents came round and said that their daughter had said something about the same teacher. All I remember is my dad, who's a lawyer, sitting in the living-room, asking me exactly what had happened. Like I was being cross-examined. He always acted like that with us. He'd be away from home for a long time and then he'd come back and behave like he was in court. I remember not being able to say anything and my younger sister answering all the questions.

My mother was one of the governors, so she went to the school and said to the teacher she'd been told that he'd been behaving improperly with the children. And he just asked if he needed to talk to his union. She replied, 'Well, don't do it again or we'll tell them.' *And that's all that happened!*

According to my sister, the abuse stopped for about six months and then started again. Anyway, the teacher left after a couple of years and got a job in another school. Shortly afterwards, he raped a little boy and got sent to prison. I suppose I felt guilty that I wasn't able to protect that boy, but I also feel angry that my parents didn't discuss what had happened to us. I remember asking my mum, 'Didn't anyone else in school notice?' and she said, 'Well...probably.' She said that another teacher had admitted to having seen this man put children on his lap – something teachers were told never to do. So, obviously, the other teacher must have suspected that something was going on and she'd blocked it out, just like my mum. I don't want to excuse them and I do feel like they all let us down. That's probably one of the reasons I went a bit wild.

The other turning point in my life was when I was thirteen. My mum was crying a lot and I asked her if Dad was having an affair, because he was away from home a lot. It turned out that Dad wasn't having an affair – she was.

Suddenly all the ideas I'd had about my parents' knowing everything disappeared and I realised they were human. It was at this point that the 'roaring' in my ears started, and it didn't stop until I was twenty-two.

★

I started to run around a lot with people I'd met at the local youth theatre. My parents told me I wasn't very nice to live with and that didn't exactly add to my self-esteem. Then, one night, I got drunk at a party and this lesbian I'd met through the group took me to someone's house and we had sex together. It was my first real sexual experience and it felt incredible. Ever since then, nothing I've ever done with a man has felt like that, yet I carried on having relationships with men because I already felt so abnormal.

At fourteen, I smoked hash for the first time and lost my virginity to this guy who was twenty-three, on speed and schizophrenic – off his rocker! He had a flat in the nearest town and I went to live with him so that I could escape my parents. I took lots of magic mushrooms and my first acid with him. We were together on and off for two years but I never felt he took care of me. In fact, I don't think I've ever felt that any of the men in my life have taken care of me.

One of the reasons I went off with this guy was that I was really ashamed of my middle-class roots, although I pretended that I wasn't. When I was at primary school the other kids were all from local farming families. My background was very different. Also, my dad was well known locally because he was involved in politics and that meant that I was kind of rejected by everyone. I felt very alienated. Then, because my dad had to be seen to be using the state system (for political reasons), I was sent to the local comprehensive. Again, I was about the only one from a middle-class background and I found it hard to mix with people.

When I got good GCSEs, my parents pushed me to go on to university. So, they sent me to a sixth-form college that was full of very rich diplomats' children. Suddenly I felt like a real hick! I went from being too posh to not being posh enough.

It was there that I started dealing hash to people. I used to cross town with 200 quids' worth of people's money and cross back with the equivalent in hash, but I never really thought of it as illegal. I just did it to make money and to make friends, because everyone else was on such massive allowances. One girl there, Sarah, used to self-harm – cut herself on her arms – and I think she had a history of being abused. Also, although her family was very rich, they were from a working-class background and I think that's why I became friends with her.

Sarah and I would get really stoned together and I used to fall asleep in class. I couldn't keep up with everyone there because, firstly, I was doing a lot of hash and, secondly, they'd all been to private schools, where standards were higher and they were taught to work harder. So I suppose I never really settled at the school. After a year of living in a girls' house, looked after by a warden – we had a curfew and everything – I said to my parents that I'd leave unless my boyfriend could come and live with me. They agreed to that but it wasn't easy, because he was still really paranoid because of all the speed he took.

Things came to a head one day when I told my boyfriend I wanted to go to a nearby festival. He refused to let me go and even locked me in the bedroom with him. I escaped through the window and walked up the road aimlessly, feeling miserable, until I came to a hospital. It had beautiful grounds behind it, with acres and acres of fields. There in one of the fields I met some travellers. Two guys. They had a caravan and a pick-up truck and they were baking Oxford Hippie Bread on the fire. Flour, salt, water, garlic – it was really nice. They were friendly and I got on especially well with one of them, Steve, who said I could travel with them. I didn't give it a second thought – I ran home, got a bag, shoved my tin whistle, some clothes, my writing book and my fiddle into it and off I went. I just dropped out of everything.

Steve used to go to these men's groups where everyone talked about their feelings and held each other and stuff. And he followed a pagan goddess-type religion, which I kind of adopted myself. The goddess has many names, from Kali to Dega, to Bridget, to Mary. A mother-earth type of thing. So, when Steve and I had sex, he couldn't penetrate me because he felt it was too disrespectful. Steve taught me a lot. He showed me how to build a bender, which is like a tent, and he was always very careful about the environment. We'd dug a fire pit and, when we left, we buried all the organic rubbish in it and replaced the turf, taking everything else with us. You couldn't tell we'd been there – there was nothing left except for a couple of tyre tracks.

After about three days with Steve, I thought maybe I should call my parents. I'd written them a letter saying I was going on the road and it was just something I felt I had to do. Unknown to me, my mum had actually spent a whole day in the city centre, looking for me and, when I phoned her she kept saying, 'Please, please come home. You've gone mad.' She was crying. It was pouring with rain and water was streaking down the outside of the phone box. It was like the whole world was crying. But I didn't go back. That was the moment I made the break, I suppose. That was when I 'crossed the line'.

We went to live in Dorset in a shared house with these people who were into making coven. Magic energies. They didn't involve me much because I was younger, but I remember there was a stream that ran by the house and they blessed it and put crystals in the water. When I walked across the bridge, it felt like I was slipping between worlds. My head was blown away with it all.

We were doing hash but I didn't see that as drugs. The main 'king' and 'queen' of the place were called Dermont and Ella and Ella was bisexual. We never got anywhere physically but I was really wound up by her and desperate for something to happen. It was Ella who first taught me to shoplift and we used to steal loads of stuff.

Then, just before Christmas, I met another traveller, Paul. He'd been on the road for about twenty years. He'd been in prison and at the Beanfield Riots, which are famous in traveller history. I went back to his bus and he didn't have any worries about the goddess, so that was all right. I spent Christmas with my parents and then went back to him. We lived together on his bus for a week or two and then he said, 'I think you should go and tell Steve what's happened and I'll pick you up in a week.' But when it came to the day we'd arranged to meet, Paul wasn't there.

I didn't know where I was going to sleep. It was about four in the afternoon and I was sitting on a bench, feeling dejected, when my dad turned up out of the blue! I'll never know how he did it, but I think he'd used his connections to find me. He knew plenty of people in the police force and just before he turned up a police car drove by. Anyway, he bought me a massive meal and then we went home to my parents' London flat, where they were now spending most of their time.

It was in London that I fell completely in love for the first time. His name was Jack and he was studying philosophy at Kings College. I soon moved in with him. But then, one day, we came back from the pub to find Paul sitting there on the steps. He'd rung my parents and my mother told him where I was. I think she thought she was doing me a favour.

Paul told me that all my belongings, which included the violin I loved so much, were on his bus, at a mate's place on the other side of London. I shouted at him for a bit and then off we went to get my stuff. Jack couldn't come with us. He had to testify in court because he'd seen an old man murdered on New Year's Eve. Halfway across London, Paul said he'd lied. My stuff was actually at his mum's in Winchester. So, we got the bus at Victoria station and twenty minutes after we set off (though we didn't know it at the time), a bomb went off at the coach station.

Everything seemed so extreme – everything was in chaos. That's what I mean when I talk about the roaring in my ears. And, of course, when I got to Winchester my fiddle wasn't there, my money wasn't there – nothing was there. All around the site, women were wearing my clothes. Paul told me he had to contact me because one of his many children was dying of leukemia and I was the only person who could comfort him. But that night he got drunk and raped me.

The next morning I managed to get back to London. I told my mum I'd been raped but she said nothing and I didn't take it any further. I suppose I just wanted to blank out the whole experience. I couldn't deal with it because my head had been so messed up by the drugs.

Two months later Jack and I were back together again and we had our own flat. Then I discovered I was pregnant. Jack and I went to the hospital for a scan and when the nurse measured the baby's head, I realised that it was too big, too well developed, to be Jack's baby. It was older, which meant that it was Paul's baby from before Christmas.

Jack and I walked home on different sides of the pavement, and it was awful. I had a baby from a man who'd raped me and Jack thought he was going to be a father and now he wasn't. So, I phoned my dad. He was so practical. He said, 'Right, we'll get a termination.' He organised it, booked it, took me along. I was quite far gone: seventeen weeks, and probably only a few days before the legal cut off. I hadn't even known I was pregnant, because I'd been doing so much speed that I wasn't really in tune with my body.

After the abortion, Jack and I rebuilt our lives but I couldn't forget the image I'd seen of my baby on the scan. I began to feel so empty and, eventually, I got pregnant again. Jack didn't want me to have the baby but I talked him into it. After the baby, Jimmy, was born we did have our good times – travelling all over Britain, an idyllic summer in Ireland with other travellers. We were on this beautiful site covered in wild flowers and herbs, the sun shone every day, all the children played together, and every night we had bonfires and parties. But I don't think Jack was ever really interested in his child. For me, the final straw came when one day Jimmy and I were laughing and playing. Jack was in bed – he was always in bed – and he just started shouting at us – 'Shut up! Shut up! I'm trying to sleep.' I said, 'Right, I've had it.' And that was it. I left him.

On site, it's quite easy to leave people because you just move into another caravan. And that's when I got it together with Brian. By now I was on self-destruct mode and that's when I crossed the line from hash to something much more serious.

With Brian I used all kinds of drugs, needles, every-thing. I was off my face for about nine months. I saw ghosts, weird things. Brian and I did a lot of acid together and one night we nearly burnt the caravan down with two kids sleeping in it. I got pregnant and came back to London, where I had another termination, also paid for by my dad. And I got into smack for three months. Really heavily. I was selling it and I didn't care. I didn't see it as illegal, I just did it. I never stopped to think, 'Ooh, I'm committing a crime.' I was just dealing with my own stuff in the best way I could.

One of the reasons I got so heavily into heroin was that Brian had raped me one night and heroin had seemed like the only way to get through it all. Nothing seemed to matter any more – I felt trapped. My sister said I had lost my spirit.

What saved me was that I got pregnant again. When I decided to keep this baby, I realised I couldn't use class A drugs anymore. Now I had someone else to think about, it gave me the courage to leave Brian. I decided to have my child alone, as a single parent, and went to live on another site with my friend, Ezra.

She was a real matriarchal type – tall and thin with three children, a massive truck and dreadlocks down to her ankles. She played the didgeridoo and drank a lot. We sort of had a relationship, but without the sex. Me and Ezra decided to do a woman's tour of Ireland. We must have been quite a sight. Me, with my tattoos and dreadlocks, her with hers, in these two massive trucks with loads of kids, pelting down the roads, pulling up in little towns, people staring. It was exciting but it was also hard work!

Then, about two weeks before my baby was born, Ezra, who had a history of abuse in her childhood, had a nervous breakdown. I was left alone in the middle of Galway, not knowing anybody, about to have my second baby. All I could do was go to the nearest site.

About two days before the baby was born, I was walking around the site when I heard someone shouting from one of the vans, 'Get out!' and I saw stuff being thrown out the door. I walked past a caravan and a woman was in there, with a social worker, trying to get her kids back. I walked past a bus and someone stamped out and shouted, 'Fuck you!' I walked past another bus. I knew the people living in it were cold turkeying from heroin. I walked past yet another and it was rattling around because people were fighting inside it. I got to my truck and just thought, I've had enough of this.

I phoned my mum and said, 'Can you come and get me when the baby is born?' and she did. I think that was the day I crossed back over the line, because the roaring in my ears stopped. I remember sitting on my bed, thinking, 'Wow, it's quiet.'

So, here I am. I came out as a lesbian a year and a half ago, and I remember thinking: Oh, God, another bloody thing to add to my list! I've got to cope with that, as well as being a single parent. But I knew I had to come out. My lesbianism is a choice and I think if someone had encouraged me to come out when I was fifteen I'd have been a lot happier. As it was, I felt really empty and broody and I think that's why I started going wild, to blot out that emptiness.

At the time, I thought it was because I wanted a baby – filling a space that I couldn't quite comprehend. I think that's crucial to a lot of teenage pregnancies. It's not always a case of mistakes or accidents. Everyone has been told in school about condoms and contraceptives. We know what we're doing.

But I've also been very, very lucky. My family never abandoned me and I was never caught for anything. If I had been, it would have affected my whole life. I would never have been able to get a clear police check every time I go for a job. I wouldn't have been allowed certain visas on a passport. If it's a drug thing, for example, you can't get into America. But I have had friends, mainly men, who have been done and I don't think prison has had any positive effect on them whatsoever. It certainly hasn't *reduced* their drug taking. In fact, it usually brings the level up. The only way for anyone to stop taking drugs is for them to say, 'I have decided I need to stop now,' and get professional help. I think that's the only thing that works.

If either of my children ever get involved with addictive drugs, I will be very worried. On the other hand, because I have been there, I think I will be a better parent. My parents were so innocent. They didn't have a clue. One of the things I really resented them for – until I became a parent and understood where they were coming from – was the fact that they didn't make me street-wise; tough enough to resist the people who took advantage of me. I think it's something I can give to my kids.

My life has been a process, a journey, and I've really grown because of the things that have happened to me. I wouldn't be who I am today without having made this journey, and I'm finally at peace with myself. I think that I am all right and I am giving a lot back. I am a good person.

Amy

I'd wanted to join the police force ever since I was thirteen. I think it was the variety of the work and the excitement that attracted me. I've no family in it or anything like that, but I couldn't imagine being tied down in an office all day.

I wanted to apply when I was eighteen, after I'd done my A levels, but I didn't think I was old enough, so I became a station reception officer for two and a half years instead. Then I applied to become a police constable. I did the entrance test – a fitness test, interview and medical – and I got through.

The job was everything I'd hoped for. You never know what you are going to get called to or what to expect. Even if you get called out for the same thing, you are dealing with different people each time and they react to you in different ways. It's exciting, which is exactly what I wanted.

Another thing that attracted me was working with

a team. When I was younger, I used to be with the Volunteer Cadet Corps. Fifteen- to nineteen-year-olds. I met quite a few friends there and I've stayed in contact with them. We did voluntary police work such as car-park duty at weekends and other stuff like that, but not everyone who was a member wanted to join the police force, it was just a social thing. We used to meet one day a week and do drill, marching, for a short while. Then we'd have an inspection and a talk about anything from jobs to family planning. The final hour was spent doing physical training. We also used to do fun things like go camping together.

Before that I was with the Guides and the Rangers. As I've said, I like teams, I like the company. You learn different things from different people and your friend-ships grow all the time.

In the police, we work together as a team. Some people imagine that we always go out in pairs, that we have a 'partner' the way they do in those American TV series, but it's not like that. Sometimes, if there's not enough manpower, you have to do things on your own. I prefer to be with a buddy because you don't know what situation you might find yourself in and I prefer to know there's someone there to help me, should I need it.

There are about twenty-three people on my team, six of whom are women. There are also two women civilians in the control room attached to our team. I trained with a hundred and forty-four other people at Hendon and there were only twenty-two women doing the course, but sexism hasn't been a problem so far. I was with one other woman in my class and when we wanted to deal with something, the boys didn't stand in our way. If we didn't want to deal with it, they'd be there. It's been the same out on the street.

The job is dangerous, of course. I've dealt with a few knife incidents and I've been called to a lot of scenes where people have pulled knives. No one has ever actually pulled a knife and threatened me with it, but when you arrive on a scene you are always aware that anything could happen – you, or a colleague, or a member of the public could get injured. But, at the time, you just deal with it. It's a job and you just get on with it.

I've been afraid many times, but it's always after everything is over and done with. I've looked back and thought, I could have been stabbed there, yet it hasn't put me off. It's like you're not yourself when you're in one of those situations – you don't have time to think, you just do your job and sort it out. Recently I was called to a scene where someone had a firearm and there were school kids everywhere. Our main concern was to get them out of the way because they wanted to see what was going on. I didn't think about the potential danger to myself until it was all over. I never think about dying. I don't think I could do the job if I did.

The bulk of my work is dealing with drink- or drug-related offences and I've had quite a bit of experience working with young people and children. Often I find myself in contact with girls of my own age or younger.

A lot of them hang about drinking in parks or grassy areas, mainly at night. Then there are the domestic incidents: women being beaten by their partners. When you're called to a house for something like domestic violence, you rarely deal only with adults. Many of these young, often very young, women have small children of their own and the children are there in the middle of it all.

A lot of women who suffer from domestic violence stay with the bloke, they don't leave him. But it can be both parties, too – women as well as men, causing domestics. And, as I've said, if it's not drug-related, then it's drink-related. What you find frequently – is that the people involved are out of work. It's connected.

I'm from north London, which isn't the area I work in, but the level of unemployment doesn't shock me. Even if you stop someone for a traffic offence you tend to find out that they're out of a job. There's a big connection between drug use and unemployment, although there are a lot of people who have got into drugs for no apparent reason. Sometimes it's simply that an older brother or sister is an addict. Cannabis is the main thing we see. Heroin, too, but mainly it's cannabis.

I've never tried drugs and I've no desire to. I drink but I don't smoke. I work out at a gym and go running. I do it for my job but also because I enjoy just getting away. It clears my head and I always feel healthier after doing a bit of sport. If you have to chase a suspect, you don't want to be lagging behind everyone else! It's especially important that you're fit because, when a suspect is running away, they have more adrenalin than you, which can give them extra speed.

I haven't been trained to use a gun and I've no desire to. We had a talk about guns, but only certain PCs use them. They never spoke to us about killing or being killed. We did watch a video once about people walking into a dangerous situation, because they wanted to get across to us that you don't know what you are going to be dealing with when you go to an incident, so you have to use caution. An apparently normal situation could turn out to be the most horrendous.

I don't know enough about the British prison system to comment on it. The only time I've been inside a prison was when I visited Holloway once but, even then, I only saw an office. I've never seen where the cells are or how the prisoners are treated. Once you arrest someone and they've been to court, you get a sheet telling you what the outcome was, whether they were sentenced, what their sentence was and so on – but that's about it. However, I do often see the ones I've arrested back out on the street. I stop and chit-chat with them, find out what they're up to, and if they have been back in again. I learn about them that way. I haven't come across any aggression towards me yet, but then I've only been to court twice so far and I don't think I've been responsible for anyone going to prison yet. The shoplifters I've arrested have been convicted and have received fines, but they haven't been given a prison sentence.

I feel the British justice system isn't backing the police

up enough and I think a lot of officers feel that. We're the ones out on the street trying to look after the victims and trying to help them. Often a criminal is released and goes straight back to target the same victim again. I don't believe in capital punishment or anything like that, but I don't think that the system as it stands works. The threat of a short prison sentence doesn't really seem to bother most criminals, because they just go and reoffend the minute they're let out, especially with things like drugs. All we can do is arrest them again. It's up to the courts after that. I believe that criminals should be given convictions for the crimes they've committed.

There was a young woman I met, my age, who had recently been released from Holloway. She reoffended. Her mum had given her her full support and said she was going to look after her. It was the perfect opportunity, but still she reoffended. She's been in prison a few times and I wonder if it's like some kind of a routine for her. She met a partner in Holloway and maybe that was why she wanted to go back in, but I just don't know.

I'm quite happy to stay on this level, on the beat. I thoroughly enjoy it. When I walk down the street in uniform, I say hello to people and they say hello to me. If I wasn't on duty and was dressed casually, I wouldn't speak to anyone I didn't know, so I suppose there is something to it, wearing a uniform. It gives you a sense of status, although it doesn't mean anything to a lot of the people you have to deal with.

All my friends respect what I do. It doesn't stand in the

way of my friendships with them. If I discovered that one of them had done something illegal, what would I do? Well, the boyfriend of my best friend takes drugs but it's nothing to do with me. It's up to him and I don't have any dealings with him. I don't want to ruin my relationship with my friend, so I don't get involved. If one of my friends was picked up for shoplifting, it wouldn't change my relationship with them, either, but I would be wary. Wary of them stealing from me and also that they might steal something while we were out. But all my friends know my position, and I don't think any of them would compromise me in that way.

Debbie

I stand on the same street corner every night, afraid, miserable, the cold wind freezing my legs, trying to outdo the other girls, yet caring about them at the same time. Every time a car slows down I feel sick and anxious. But I need the money. This degrading humiliation is the only way.

People who drive past look at me as if I'm dirt. They think I'm a slut, but what do they know? It's easy when the good things in life are handed to you on a plate. They don't realise how it feels, how much it hurts, when people turn away from you as if you're nothing.

I have to work. I have a baby to fight for and a drug habit to feed. If I don't make money, I'll never get a place to live and I'll never get my baby back. But I also need my heroin. I'm not proud of it – I pray with each car that slows down that my baby will never know I did this. I pray she'll never have to stand here herself, even though my mum stood here before me.

★

When I was young my father left my mum and me to fend for ourselves. We ended up in a tiny flat over a chip shop that smelt greasy all the time but it was all Mum could afford. She used to say of an evening, 'I'm off to work to keep us all,' and I never asked where she went – you don't when you're young, do you? Like you never ask why your dad hits you, or why he falls over breaking things, or why your mum is bruised and miserable. Mum always looked so worn and tired, too tired for life.

My dad betrayed me and my mother. He touched me in places he never should have and that's why I ended up taking speed. To start off with, I just took it now and again, but I couldn't get rid of the burning anger inside me. Somehow that anger helps me through the difficult times. I'm angry with Mum, too – she betrayed me because she let it happen – but it's hard to hate your mum.

I'm only twenty-two but I feel like I've lived a hundred years. There was never anything worthwhile in my life until I met Pete, and we had the baby, our little girl. She's all I want, my life, my reason for living. Pete didn't stick around – he got violent and left us. He's inside now.

Sometimes I fantasise about what life would be like if Pete hadn't left. We'd all be home together, like one of those families you see in the shopping precinct or the cinema.

It's strange watching those other families. I see one of my clients walking around the precinct with his wife and little girl, all hand in hand. He and his wife love each other, you can see that from the way they look at each other. She'd die of hurt if she knew he'd been with a prostitute. The betrayal of trust is the worst thing. Another guy comes to me because his wife is dying and he spends the whole time sobbing. It makes me think, why do any of us do these things?

My priority is getting my baby back. She'll be walking soon, cutting her back teeth. I'm only allowed to visit her once a week at the moment and I hate seeing her in her foster mother's arms. She's mine. I have to save up to keep her, so I need the strength to say no to heroin. It makes you so horrible, it destroys you.

I still have dreams. I wanted to do A levels, settle down, but I haven't had much of a chance in life so far. I've only had betrayal – my dad, my mum, my boyfriend, the dealers – but never any love. It's so cold in this world, no warmth for a prostitute addicted to heroin. All I want is a hug, not sex, but a real human hug – the sort that tells me I'm a person with a brain and a heart. I want to know I'm loveable.

Catherine

I've been in prison for a month, on remand. I'm here because I got involved with drugs and the wrong sort of people. I did a favour for a friend and got caught taking drugs into another prison. That's what happens when you do a friend a favour. I didn't even know the bloke I was going to visit.

I'm from Yorkshire originally and I left home when I was sixteen. I had a problem with my parents. My mother was very domineering and we used to argue a lot. Dad never used to say anything when I was upset, even though I wanted him to. He just kept his mouth shut.

After that, wherever I lived, I felt insecure. I felt I wasn't loved. I felt out of place. I spoke to my nan about it and she thinks it's because my parents didn't show me enough love when I was younger. My father is affectionate, but my mother never used to show her feelings or emotions in front of anyone. She's a very hard woman.

But you can't really blame it on your parents, not really...

The person I smuggled the drugs into the prison for, Tommy, was also from Yorkshire. He was a friend from my home town and one of my best girlfriends was going out with him. He had just come out of prison after serving four years for armed robbery and he wanted to get some drugs to a friend who was still inside, but didn't want to risk getting caught. He said I'd be all right because no one would suspect me.

I think one of the reasons I agreed to do it was that I found all the violence quite exciting. I was stupid, foolish, I suppose. If Tommy didn't want to take the drugs in, then it was because there was a risk of being caught.

Tommy gave me the drugs outside the prison, just before I went in. They were in a little plastic bag. I thought – or so my girlfriend told me – that it was only going to be some cannabis but, in fact, it was a little bit of heroin and a few sleeping tablets as well. I put the bag down my trousers and hid it in my vagina. I was searched externally when I entered the prison but they didn't find anything. I thought I had got away with it.

When we were in the visitor's room, I got up and went to the bathroom, pulled the packet out of my vagina, hid it in my clenched hand, went back out and sat down opposite the prisoner. I was about to hand the bag over to him – you know, you put your hand on the table and he puts his on top, as though you are just making contact with each other – but before I could do that, the wardens came over to where we were both sitting and circled me. I was really worried and started to cry.

Someone must have grassed the bloke up. The prison wardens had obviously been alerted that drugs were coming in and they were waiting for me. The prison knew I was coming, basically.

They didn't arrest me there and then. They just took my name and address and told me to go home. That's why I thought that nothing was going to come of it.

All this was before I met my boyfriend. I was smuggling drugs into a prison even though I'd never taken drugs myself. I was clean. But that was soon to change.

I'd only been living in south Yorkshire for a few months. One night I was in a club with some friends and I met this guy. We got on really well and I ended up going out with him. He told me that he'd lived in London and had come to south Yorkshire to sort his life out and make a fresh start. At the time I thought he'd left London because he'd split up with his girlfriend (they had a child together). It wasn't until about a month later that he told me he'd just come out of prison after doing four years for burglaries and drug-related crimes. He had a problem with crack and cocaine.

He kept telling me that prison had sorted his life out and he'd changed. That's why I fell in love with him. You know, I believed it. You do when you're in love, don't you? You're blind. It wasn't long before I moved in with him. I was only eighteen and he was twenty-six, much older than me.

It was my boyfriend who introduced me to heroin. Before I met him, I'd smoked a little bit of cannabis but never anything heavy. We were sitting around with this friend of his, who was a dealer, and they offered me some. I didn't think at the time. All I knew was that a lot of my friends had taken it and said it was amazing. So I tried it, and I liked it.

It never takes long to become addicted to heroin, especially if you are living with someone who has a habit. Once my boyfriend and I moved in together, we started taking it regularly. It was expensive. My addiction was about a gram a day, which costs about £70 or £80. His was a bit more. We were trying to support nearly £200 worth of drug addiction a day.

It was around this time, six months after I'd taken the drugs into the prison for Tommy, that the police showed up at my work and arrested me. I lied about it to my boss because I couldn't tell him it was drug related. I told him that my boyfriend had stolen a car and that was why the police had wanted to question me. My boss was fine and didn't sack me.

Down at the police station, I was too frightened to say that I'd been put up to smuggling the drugs into the prison. I didn't want to get my head kicked in. I took the rap for it, one hundred per cent, because I was too frightened not to.

The police told me that they were letting me go home for the moment, but I would be sent a court date and it was vital that I attend. The reason I'm here in prison now is that I missed that date because my boyfriend started beating me up.

By now, we were taking heroin every day. We were

getting up every morning, taking it and then trying to find enough money to buy more. Within weeks, I was too ill to work. If I took the day off, I had to make up excuses. The truth was, I was just too ill to travel the ten miles to work and I needed the time to steal so that we'd have enough money to buy heroin. I also told myself that I just wanted to hang around with my boyfriend. I did realise that the relationship might not be healthy but I was so into drugs by then that I couldn't see straight. Finally, the choice became between him and heroin, or work. I chose him.

The first time he beat me up, it wasn't that bad. I went back to him because I loved him. Then it got worse and worse. To start with, it was just a punch in the face but then it got to the point where I was actually lying on the floor being kicked. He beat my face, my arms, everything. He bruised my stomach and ribs, kicking me in the back. It happened when he was angry, because we didn't have the money to buy drugs.

I tried leaving him but I kept going back because I loved him. I thought that if I could get the money to satisfy his addiction, it would all be fine. I even went round to my grandparents and asked them for money which was something I'd never done before. My grand-parents realised something was up. They asked me there and then, 'Are you on drugs?' And I told them, 'No.' My boyfriend was with me and he said that we needed the money for the deposit on a flat. They lent me £150 and we spent it all on one day's habit.

My sisters knew he was beating me. They told my nan that I was into drugs and she started to write to me regularly, trying to help. But my boyfriend said, 'Just forget about your family. Let's get on with us.'

The reason I forgot my court date was that I finally ran away from him. I'd had enough. I just left everything, all my stuff, at his place and ran. But the letters about the court case were also in his flat. So, that's why I am in here. I simply forgot the date while I tried to sort out somewhere safe to live and I was arrested. It was a committal to crown court and I missed the date...

The probation board are trying to bring my case forward. They think I'm going to get out on a probation order because I've never been in trouble with the police before. I've also got in touch with my family. My uncle says I can stay at his caravan site when I get out and he's going to come to court with me. That's important because they won't let me out of prison if I don't have an address to go to. I don't think my parents would have me back. My mum wrote me a terrible letter a few days after I first came here. She said she was disgusted with me and what I'd done was a shock for all the family. But the letters are beginning to get better now and I think Mum respects me because I told my little sister that leaving home was the worst mistake of my life.

I've also split up with my boyfriend. I don't want to see him again, but it took being in prison to make me realise that. When I first came here I was so upset that I kept ringing him, saying, I love you and I want to see you.

Now, I think of all the times he beat me up and I hate him. He hasn't tried to contact me and I think he might be back in prison himself. He was on an electronic tag when I came to prison because he kept getting done for driving offences, even after he'd been banned.

I haven't spoken to Tommy, the bloke I did the favour for, and my other friends since my arrest because I want to get rid of that side of my life. All the people I used to hang about with base their lives on drugs and that's something I don't want to be involved with any more.

Drugs are a vicious circle. Once you get hooked, it's hard to get out. It's such a shame that it's taken all this to make me see sense. I suppose one of the main reasons I took drugs was to cover up my personal problems. But then, problems don't go away. They are still there the next day.

I always felt that my parents didn't encourage me enough. I got all my GCSEs and went to college to do my A levels; law, business studies and English. I did a year and a half and then my mum talked me into moving back home and getting a job. They didn't need the money and I think Mum was jealous because she never got the opportunity to go to college herself. My father just kept his mouth shut because whatever my mum says, goes.

I wouldn't dare bring all this up with her now. It's a very closed subject. But I am going back to college to get my A levels – business, English and probably psychology. Before all of this happened I wanted to be a solicitor but I can't really do law any more. To tell you the truth, I can't think much beyond my A levels at the moment, but when I get out of prison I'm going to do what *I* want, not what anyone else tells me to do. I'm going to succeed in life and make my own decisions.

Sweet Pea

My father was in England for a few months, visiting his
brothers and sisters, and I decided to come over and see
him. It was to have been a surprise for Father's Day but
it didn't turn out as I had planned.

I'm from Kingston, Jamaica, and I'd never been to
England before. Back home I was having a lot of personal
problems, concerning my family. I'm eighteen, the
youngest in the family, and I have two brothers and three
sisters. My mother died when I was thirteen. I confided
in a good friend about my problems and he offered to
help me out by buying me an air ticket to London to see
my father.

This friend was someone I trusted. I had known him
for years. So when he offered to pay for the ticket, I
thought it was purely a gesture of friendship. I didn't find
it strange when he introduced me to another of his
friends, who wanted me to take something to England
for him. This friend gave me a canister of hairspray and

said it was for a cousin of his. At the time, I believed him. It didn't occur to me that there could be anything else in the canister.

I was caught at the airport. Customs stopped me. I was looking for my luggage and I needed help to get it off the conveyor belt because it was heavy. One of the customs officers said she'd help me, and then she started to check through my bags. First, she asked me all the routine questions – did I have anything to declare and so on. I said no. Then she did an X-ray on the can of hairspray. The customs people told me the can contained 183 grams of cocaine. I had no idea.

After I was arrested, the police drove me to the local station and took my fingerprints and my picture. I hadn't tried to make contact with the cousin and I gave the police all the information. It was a weekend so I had to stay in the station until Monday, when they took me to court. After the preliminary hearing, they drove me to this prison. It was all very scary. I'd never been in trouble with the police before. I don't even smoke, let alone take drugs.

I have to go to court on 2 September to plead guilty or not guilty. I'm not guilty. I didn't know what was in that can and my solicitor thinks I have a good chance of getting off. My first solicitor wasn't really doing anything, so someone in the office here told me about HIBISCUS, and they helped me apply for legal aid so that I could find a more suitable solicitor.

HIBISCUS is an organisation for girls from Jamaica and the Caribbean. A team from HIBISCUS comes here every Monday to see us during 'Activities' and a woman from the team visits me regularly. HIBISCUS watches over you, they help you find solicitors and barristers, pay for the costs or help you do the paperwork for legal aid. When you want to get in contact with your family, they help out. If it is too expensive to phone home, they will send money to buy phonecards.

I haven't asked HIBISCUS for money to call home because I have a job here in prison at the Reed work centre. I get paid £1.40 for stuffing one hundred envelopes. The money goes into a personal account and it has paid for all my phonecards so far, although it is only about £6 a week and one phonecard is £5. I never see the actual money. We are not given it, just told how much we have to spend. Sometimes, I have enough for what I need, sometimes not. My father gives me a little bit of money, but I don't like to trouble him.

I don't want my father to come to the court hearing. He is very upset. He comes to see me here about once a week, but he will only be in England for another month or two. My aunts and uncles have also visited me and I guess they'll continue to be supportive. I don't know. Apart from them and my family in Jamaica, no one knows I'm in prison. Back in Jamaica, I have a lot of friends, but I haven't spoken to any of them because I don't want them to know where I am. My father said to me, 'I guess you know who your real friends are now,' and he's right. He didn't know the friend who set me up because I don't usually introduce friends to my family, but he knows that I am innocent.

I'm spending my time here doing word processing, pottery, arts and crafts, and that's basically it. I was studying for my A levels back home – tourism management and psychology – but I've missed out on a lot of school. I had been preparing for university and I still hope to be able to go.

When I first came here two months ago, I was put in a cell by myself but now I am in a dorm. I haven't made friends here and I don't really want to. I find it a bit scary. I cry at night and I feel so isolated. The whole experience has opened my eyes up to a world I didn't know existed. I hope I get off. I'm lonely and I want to go home.

Since this first interview with Sweet Pea, her case has been heard and she has been found guilty. She was sentenced to three years and nine months in prison, which means that she will serve half of that sentence here in England and then will be deported back to Jamaica.

My father has returned to Jamaica now. I phone him every week. My uncle, his brother, still visits regularly.

Since I arrived here the system has changed. This prison now has a separate block for young offenders, which means that once you are sentenced you don't have to be moved on to another prison. I don't like the young offenders' block, though, I preferred the other wing. The wardens were less rigid.

I still maintain my innocence. I consider the British justice system unjust because the guilty walk out of here free and the innocent are left behind.

Emily

I have been at a private, mixed boarding-school in the west of England since the age of seven. This was a result of my parents' divorce. I am an only child and, up until that major change in my life, I had been the centre of attention for both my parents. It was, in fact, too much attention because both parents were attempting to protect me from each other. But nothing could compensate for the eruption that took place inside me when they split up.

We were once a close family but it is hard for me to remember that now. From a very early age, I had to cope with situations that no child should ever have to deal with. Spending my childhood in a boarding-school seemed very unnatural – a controlled, protected environment but at the same time one that appeared hostile and alien to me. I had been pulled from a place where I felt safe and loved, separated from my parents who I was used to seeing every day, and pushed into a situation that I was not prepared for.

In my bewildered state, I made some dubious friend-
ships, and found myself being dragged into difficult
situations by a girl who appeared to be stronger than I was.
Once or twice my involvement with this girl led me to the
point of being expelled. But, in the midst of all this, I had
also made a group of firm friends who were very valuable
to me, although at the time I did not realise it.

Through all these incidents in my early school life
there was one girl, Rebecca, who was always there to put
me back on the right track. She was the one who made
me realise what this other girl was doing to my life. As a
result, I finally managed to disentangle myself from that
situation and from then on I began to enjoy my school
life more.

Time went on and, with the change from prep school
to senior school, Rebecca and I began to drift apart.
Although we still remained good friends, we had now
entered separate groups and were involved with our new
friends. It was not until several years later, when we were
sixteen, that I realised she had become involved with
the wrong type of people. She was in trouble, and it was
my turn to help her, just as she had helped me many
years back.

The cause of my concern was drugs, and I had a gut
feeling that Rebecca was in deep. She changed her
appearance and began to wear clothes that she thought
were 'cool'. At first, no one said anything, as it was up to
her what she wore but, gradually, she began to look
worse, as if she didn't care about herself at all. She stopped
washing regularly and never wore any make-up. She

began to see the things that she had done before, such as shopping, going to the cinema, just chatting or having a good laugh, as 'sad'. Instead, she would go for a spliff. She had always been intelligent and excelled in both the academic and athletic sides of school, but these deteriorated rapidly with her habit. Her language also changed. All she could talk about was how she and her mates were going to take speed and E that Saturday night. It got to the point where she was almost boasting about it. She thought it was the cool thing to do. I don't think she realised that everyone else didn't think it was 'cool' at all. No one could believe how much she'd changed.

Rebecca and her group shut everyone out of their lives. They were interested solely in themselves and no one was allowed to penetrate their tight circle unless they, too, were into drugs. I think they felt that anyone who did not take drugs was uncool, and they could not have that sort of person damaging their reputation.

I tried talking to Rebecca. In fact, the conversation I had with her is still vivid in my memory. I remember trying to make her see sense. I said, 'Rebecca, how can you take E or anything else without thinking about whether you'll live to remember it?' Her reply was, 'For fuck's sake, why can't you just leave it alone? It's up to me if I want to take drugs and, anyway, I trust the bloke I get them from.' I suppose it was easier to say something like that rather than face the facts.

After that, I realised it was only a matter of time before she and her druggy mates got caught. They were becoming reckless and were now smoking spliffs whenever they could – in their lunch breaks, after school, all the time – and it was becoming really obvious. At the weekends they would take a wide range of drugs. Base, E, speed. Anyone could tell from the way they looked that they were on something.

Then it happened, the moment we had all been expecting. 'The crowd' decided to go away for a weekend and they obviously thought it was a good opportunity to take drugs without getting caught. It just so happened that one of the people driving left a spliff in their car and when their parents came to clean the car out they found it. These parents rang the school and told them about the drugs and who had been away on the weekend. The rest of us could only sit back, watch the ordeal our friends had to go through and be there to support them when they needed it – which was often.

The news spread fast, as some heartless student told the press, and so within days the information had spread to the radio and newspapers. I think the sheer humiliation of being in the papers for such a reason helped Rebecca to realise her mistakes. She thought she would never get caught, it would never happen to her. Drugs seem to do that to you. They give you a false sense of security and the illusion of invincibility.

Gradually, the incident died down and the press soon moved on, but Rebecca now had to have regular drug tests to make sure she no longer took drugs. She once said that she felt confined and constantly watched by the teachers in our school as she no longer had their trust. Even though the rest of them still took drugs during the holidays, they took them less and less until it was just the occasional spliff. Rebecca never spoke about how her parents reacted to the situation but I have the feeling that their constant reprimandings must have been a great strain.

Rebecca is gradually returning to the friend I once related to, although time and this incident have damaged the friendship we once had. She cares about her appearance and, although she is still involved with her friends, they have all begun to take an interest in other people; people who don't take drugs. Despite the fact that we all wish that it hadn't taken them being caught for this change to occur, it has altered their outlook on life and that is a good thing. In fact, just the other day, I was speaking to Rebecca about the past two years of our sixth form and how in individual ways we had wasted our time and she said: 'I realise now that if I hadn't taken drugs, I wouldn't be as behind in my work and I wouldn't have lost the friends that I did.'

Angela

My name is Angela and I was born and brought up in Wales. I was nineteen when I went to jail. Although my sentence was one year, I only had to serve six months, but there were two and a half years between the original charge and the conviction. It was an awful time for me and for my family – I didn't even tell my parents or my older brother until about three or four months after I was arrested. I had a good job as a book-keeper in a well-respected firm, but I started stealing money by fiddling the books. It was a vast sum. I stole £24,500 over a period of less than a year. I didn't do it for myself. I gave the money to my boyfriend to stop him beating me.

It sounds strange, but my boyfriend and I met at some traffic lights. A friend and I were driving home from the sports centre, where we'd been to an aerobics class. We got to some lights and they were red. Suddenly the two guys in front of us got out of their car and started to walk towards us. Not knowing what they wanted, we reversed our car and locked the doors but we'd left the windows open. It could have been a sticky situation but actually they just wanted to chat us up. I got talking to one of them, Victor, and was completely overwhelmed by him. We started seeing each other and, altogether, I knew him for nearly two years.

Victor had a lot of problems. His real mother had died of cancer and his father was in prison. He didn't seem to know why and I think he was probably very young when his father went in. When he was seven, he was adopted by a well-to-do doctor's family.

There were two sides to Victor. He had notions of grandeur because he had been brought up by a wealthy family but, inside, he felt he came from nothing. He used to take drugs and I think he had a criminal record, because of his attitude towards the police, but he never said anything about it.

I'd known him for about six or seven months (by now we were living together), when he saw this car for sale. It was a VW Beetle, and he really wanted it. He kept mentioning it, and then saying that he would never be able to get a bank loan, that he could never afford it. Then he began pushing on me, you know, asking me whether I could get a loan, or some form of credit. We started to have arguments because I couldn't understand why he wanted it so badly – he already *had* a Beetle. I asked him, 'Why go for this one, when you already have one?' That's when he first hit me. He pushed me up against a door, punched my nose and broke it. He kept punching and kicking me for ten, fifteen minutes.

When he saw the state he'd left me in he took me to the hospital. It was Friday night and the place was packed. There was even a couple of police waiting at reception. I nearly died of embarrassment. I couldn't bring myself to tell anyone what had really happened so I told the hospital that I'd been jumped, mugged. Victor was going to call my parents. I said, 'Are you mad? You'll be the next one with a broken nose!' I felt ashamed of what had happened and I was frightened – too frightened to tell even my family.

Anyway, less than a week later, I gave Victor the money for the car. He didn't question it, didn't ask me where it had come from. He didn't know I'd embezzled it. I think he believed my parents were rich. The point was, he was happy, and when he was happy, he wasn't beating me.

I started fiddling the books at work on a regular basis just to give Victor money and make him feel good. He hadn't asked me to steal but I couldn't take the physical abuse and I lacked the self-confidence just to get up and leave him. I suppose I was also obsessed with him. I don't know if it was love, but I don't think so. If I had thought more of myself I wouldn't have needed to keep putting him first. I don't know how many times I thought I should leave, but I never did.

There were times when he beat me for the stupidest things, like not wearing make-up. I never did wear a lot of cosmetics in those days. I'd never seen my mum put on a face, so I had no confidence in how to do it. Then Victor threw out all my knickers and made me wear some big ones that he'd bought. There were only three women working in my office and all the rest were men. Looking back on it, I think Victor was afraid that someone else would go for me, so he made me wear those huge knickers and forbade me from wearing skirts. In fact, it's only in the last two years that I've found the confidence to stop wearing trousers all the time and begin to wear skirts again.

Victor kept buying all these things with the money I gave him. The place was chock-a-block with possessions but still he didn't know I was embezzling. Then I got caught.

I had taken a week's holiday from work and decided to spend one of the days visiting my parents. When I arrived at their place – I remember I was carrying this little puppy I had – they told me that my boss had telephoned, looking for me. I knew then. A kind of sixth sense told me that he had found out. I spoke to him on the phone and he said he wanted to see me right away because the accountant had been looking at the books and there were a few irregularities. So, I went to see him with the puppy still in my arms (my parents had two big dogs and I didn't want to leave it with them). My boss told me that he wasn't going to allow me to leave the office and that he was phoning the police.

I wanted to get out of there and think things through, because the shit was about to hit the fan big time. I suddenly remembered a story from my father's workplace, where one of the men had stolen the wages. My father couldn't forcibly hold him. He'd had to wait for the police. So, I told my boss he couldn't forcibly hold me, that he didn't have the right to do it. He said, 'I see you have been in trouble before.' I said, 'No, but I want to leave. You can call the police and they can come and arrest me but, right now, I am walking out of here.' And I did, still holding the damn dog. I was shaking all over.

When I got home I didn't say anything to Victor, except that I'd lost my job because my boss had asked me to work during my week off and I had refused.

The police came four or five days later on the Saturday morning. The bell rang and Victor didn't answer it. He never answered the door unless he was expecting someone. Instead he went out on to the fire exit to see who was there. When he came back he told me the police were there. It was only then that I told him what had happened. He went ballistic, and warned me that on no account was I to tell the police what I had been doing with the money. I was arrested and taken down the station. And I just came clean straight away. I knew I was in enough trouble already and it was time to tell the truth. It felt like such a relief to finally get it off my chest. That's why I wanted to tell my story here. To get it all out.

The police charged me and took my fingerprints. They accused me of being a drug user, of buying drugs with all the money, but I told them it wasn't that. Anyway, once they had all my details they sent me home, saying that I would be hearing from them. When I got back to the flat Victor beat me up and locked me out. The irony is that some of the money I'd stolen went towards paying for that very flat and I think that Victor is still living there now. But, even when my curiosity is riding high, I never try to find out if he is there. I just want him to rot in hell.

The two and a half years between being charged and being convicted were very hard on my family. Both my parents' fathers were policemen and the story was in all the local papers. Because of my upbringing, I've always presented myself well, so when I went to court, I dressed up in a suit. I'm not sure if it made any difference at the time, but I do know that the way you look can alter the way people react to you.

My background made prison life very difficult. I was singled out because I was different. But the governor of the prison was terrific. He had a daughter my age, and I think he identified with me and with my parents. He always came to see them, to say hello and find out how they were coping. After I left prison, he would phone and ask me how I was getting on. Nothing untoward. He just wanted to see how I was doing. Although it was a real culture shock for my parents, they now call that time 'when Angela was in the convent' or, sometimes, 'Angela's sabbatical'.

Now I just want to get on with my life. I have been living in a different town, alone, with my cat and dog. I never see Victor. When I answer the phone, if someone asks for me and I don't recognise their voice, I pretend that I am 'Angela's sister', even though I don't have a sister. I do it just in case it's someone I don't want to talk to. But the main news is that I am moving to England in a few weeks to live with this really kind guy. He was a friend to me during my troubles, although we didn't form a relationship until recently. He knows all about Victor, but never judged me, and he is always very supportive. We really love each other.

Nowadays, I don't allow people to belittle me. I feel happy and positive about my future and I have discovered a confidence in who I am and how I look. I know that many people who have committed crimes are not as fortunate, and I am truly grateful for the way things have turned out and the support I have been given.

Ella

I'm eighteen. I've been in prison for three weeks for shoplifting. I already had a criminal record. I was stealing to feed my drug habit. What can I tell you? I was placed on a care order because of neglect and abuse and I have spent my life fending for myself.

At fourteen, I fell pregnant, became a drug user and basically my baby was taken into care. I was obliged to hand her over to social services when she was only six and a half months old. They came in here to see me recently. They said they had found parents to adopt her and they wanted me to sign the papers, but I wouldn't sign them. I want to get my baby back, when all of this mess is cleared up. ·

I think my boyfriend was the start of all my problems. Well, my drug problem, at least. Basically, he got me into drugs and started me offending. I was only thirteen when I met him and I was on heroin by the time I was fourteen. My boyfriend's sister was a dealer and he was helping her, but he was also an addict himself.

When the baby was born, my boyfriend couldn't live up to his responsibilities and he left. He knows he has a little girl but he won't have anything to do with her. I'm glad he's gone.

My other problems started long before that. I was in the care system from the age of three until I was fourteen. I went from children's homes to foster homes, back to children's homes and then to foster homes again. I was moved from pillar to post the whole time. Fifteen different moves.

I was on a care order for neglect and abuse right up until last month. When I was younger my mum neglected me and my sisters, and my grandad abused us. I don't remember much about it at all. For a while, I used to go home at weekends and stay with Mum, but it didn't work out. Then Mum went into prison for defrauding social security. She had been trying to get money to feed us all.

There are seven of us in the family altogether. One brother is through incest, because my mum was raped by her dad, my grandad, and from that she had a little boy – he's my eldest brother. I still see him from time to time and we get on quite well now, although we didn't when we were younger. There are also two other sisters from my dad and another woman – they live with my aunties. We're a big family.

My dad died when I was two. I've never seen a photo of him and I don't remember him at all. I've been told that when I was little I was very ill and had to stay in hospital for a while and my dad was there with me every night and every day.

My mum now lives in Manchester, but she used to live in Croydon, which is why I ended up going down there. I stayed with her for a while but, when she moved back to Manchester, I decided to hang on and see if I could make another go of it by myself. Things didn't turn out well.

I have a twenty-seven-year-old sister who lives in Croydon and she has her own family and her own house. But because she's got children and responsibilities, I couldn't stay there. So, I had to find other places to sleep. Occasionally my sister-in-law gave me a bed so I could get my head down but that wasn't always possible. At some points, I was sleeping on the streets. Then I stayed in a squat for a while. It was my mum's old address, actually, but it belonged to the council and when they found out, they moved everyone out. There was nothing left. They took all our clothes, everything.

When I was caught shoplifting I was brought in here, and they put me straight into detox. I went through my first detox programme a couple of months ago but, soon afterwards, I bumped into an old friend and got into heroin again. So, as soon as I arrived back here in jail, I went into detox again. They won't allow you on the landing or on the young offenders' wing unless you are clean. The detox I went through took ten days. I don't remember much about it, but it was all right, actually. Not that bad.

Although all of my brothers and sisters still communicate, none of them have come to visit me here – it's too far. My mum hasn't been, either, but I don't really expect her to come all the way from Manchester. It's too expensive and it's a long way. Anyway, Mum's sick, she's got angina. She's had two or three heart attacks already and I think she's only forty-five. She's been married to this bloke up in Manchester but she's going to divorce him. He's got leukemia. I used to think of him as a stepdad and I was quite fond of him. Whenever I go back to Manchester, I go to visit him. Even though he's not living with my mum anymore, he's still family.

I've made one or two friends here. The girl in the bed next to me comes from Croydon and I knew her before I came in. I met two of the other girls the last time I was in prison. They're all right. No one frightens or upsets me here. The staff are all right, too. The screws, the officers, are good if I need someone to talk to.

I'm not shocked by being here because I've been in prison twice before – both times for the same thing. Each time I was sentenced to two months but I only served one. At the time I was still under eighteen, so I was under a supervision order, which meant I could only get probation if there was a responsible adult to look after me. Mum and my stepdad lived too far away for that. I did ask my stepdad to go to the court to get the supervision order dropped, but he said it wouldn't work because we didn't live in the same place.

Now that I'm eighteen things are different. The

probation people came to see me and said that I have a chance of a walk-out because I have already done three weeks on remand, waiting to be sentenced. In the court's eyes that's like six weeks, so they may say that I've done enough time already.

I'm being sentenced tomorrow. Whether I get a walk-out or not, I'll probably only be in this prison for a couple more days, because it's an adult prison. They keep you here on remand but, once you've been sentenced, you only go back to an adult prison if you are over twenty-one or if no other prison will accept you. I heard the place they'll probably send me to is a shit-hole. But if you can do one jail, you can do another. That's the way I see it.

If I'm lucky and I get a walk-out, I'll go back to Manchester to fight for my baby. I'll live with one of my other sisters. Ever since social services came in with the adoption papers, I've been determined to make a go of it and not go back on drugs. That's when it really sank in: I could lose my baby. I want to go back and make a new life. I've got to do it, really. I'll do it for myself and my baby.

Lara

I'm not guilty. I shouldn't be here. I got three years for GBH.

What happened was I went out one night with my cousin and another girl we didn't know very well – we'd only spoken to her a few times. We went to McDonald's and she started an argument with one of the girls she knew there. My cousin and I left because the manager said that if we didn't go, he'd phone the police. So we left, and waited for the girl outside.

Then we all went to a different McDonald's because we still hadn't had anything to eat. This girl started another argument outside with someone else she knew and, well, she got into a fight and used a knife.

We fell out after that. She kept saying she'd used a knife, how she'd done this and she'd done that, and I didn't like it. I had nothing to do with her fights. But two months later, the police came to my door. I was arrested and brought in to be interviewed. The police told me that the two of them, my cousin and this girl, had said it was me who had used the knife. So, I went through everything, told them about the other McDonald's, about the girl shouting at the manager there. I just told the truth. From what I told them, they were able to gather a load of evidence against the girl and everything I said was confirmed by witnesses.

I thought that left me and my cousin in the clear, but the police said they thought we knew about the knife, which made us accomplices. The case went through magistrates, then to the crown court. I told my solicitor and the barrister about another incident that had happened about a month after the first. My cousin and this girl were both out together. They got into an argument with someone, and a knife was used again. But I wasn't there – it was just them. I mentioned it to my defence because I thought it would prove that I wasn't the one making trouble. So, the court brought the other case in with this one and my cousin and the other girl were tried for the two offences together.

At first we all said not guilty, but then the girl who'd used the knife changed. She said she was guilty so that she wouldn't have to sit through the trial. Me and my cousin still said not guilty, and we had to go through the whole process.

I was always told I'd be acquitted because of all the evidence, the help I'd given and the way I'd come across in court. But when it came to the last day of the hearing, when all the evidence was summed up and they announced the jury's findings, I was found guilty. They found my cousin guilty as well.

I was brought here, to prison, for three weeks, then taken back to court for sentencing. I was sentenced to three years, and my cousin, who's got three children, to six. The girl who actually used the knife both times only got three and a half years. That was the judge's decision, because he didn't believe she'd used the knife the second time, he thought it was my cousin. The witnesses who'd seen it happen were in court, but they didn't say anything against the other girl. During the trial, my cousin's barrister stood up and asked them, 'Isn't it true you've had contact with the girl since?' They said, 'Yes'. Then, when he asked, 'Can you tell me what was said?', they all started crying. They didn't want to say anything more about her – she wasn't the sort of girl you messed with. Still, in spite of this, the judge blamed my cousin for the second attack.

I was sentenced a week before my baby was due. I wasn't in a relationship at the time of the incident but, a month later, I started going out with this guy, and then we moved in together. When I first met him, he knew what had happened and what the other girl had done, because she'd been bragging about it. This guy supported me all the way through the trial and I became pregnant about a month after moving in with him.

Nobody ever thought I'd have to go to prison, so I didn't do anything about the baby. But if I'd known I was going to end up in jail, I would have taken something, I wouldn't have gone ahead with the pregnancy.

Me and my boyfriend had always wanted a big family because we both came from one ourselves. But, when it came to the time for me to give birth, I had to have a Caesarean because I was so stressed. That means I might not be able to have more than three children.

Since I've been in here, I've been in such a state, crying all the time, that I've started seeing a psychiatrist. This is my first time in trouble with the law and it's such a shock. The other two have had dealings with the police before, but not me. I'd thought that would make a difference with the judge but it didn't.

A lot of people might have expected me to have been in trouble before because I'd lived in a children's home. I was there because of my parents. They weren't my real mum and dad and I never really felt that they accepted me. When my real mum was pregnant with me, she met another man and had two children with him. She got divorced from him and took the youngest child with her but left me and my sister with our stepdad. I was only three at the time and I haven't heard from my mum since. My stepdad then married a woman who had two children from a previous marriage. They have been together ever since and have had two more children of their own, but you can see why I never felt I belonged. Things got bad and I ended up in the care system.

When I had my baby son, Brian, my stepmum and dad and my sister never bothered coming to the hospital. They seem to have turned against me. They're telling stories about my boyfriend that aren't true and they're causing a lot of problems between me and him.

It's not as if they couldn't come and see me, either – I've got a little stepsister who's in here and my stepmum visits her. She was always wild and everyone said she would end up in prison one day. She's only seventeen but she's already got over ten charges on her. Theft and TDA (taking and driving away a stolen vehicle), no insurance, no tax. She's also got a nine-month-old baby.

My boyfriend is really depressed. He's stopped working and he's lost a lot of weight. But he's got to come to terms with my prison sentence. I've got to come to terms with it, too. And, when the time comes, he'll have to look after our baby. Brian could stay with me in prison for eighteen months but I am handing him over to his dad at the end of nine months because, if I wanted to keep him longer, then I'd have to go to a prison in Manchester, and that's too far away. His dad wouldn't be able to visit us or take him out.

The other reason I don't want my baby to be here is the drugs. My boyfriend was really worried and I tried to play the drugs problem down, but the other day there was a big scene when one of the visitors was caught smuggling drugs in and my boyfriend saw it all.

It's been a shock being around so many drugs and so much violence. That's one of the reasons I don't talk to the other girls much. I don't want to get involved with the drug taking and the bullying that goes on. All sorts of things. I just want to look after my baby, get on with my life and go home.

My barrister thinks there's low grounds for an appeal but my solicitor has advised me to get another legal team. He thinks I should appeal, because there's new evidence. The other girl has written a letter saying I wasn't involved. If she'd done that before I got convicted, I wouldn't be in here today, but her barrister wants her to withdraw the letter. There's definitely something wrong somewhere and I'm going to see if I can get a retrial.

Before I came in here I had so many plans. I was going to have my baby and then go back to college to do my GCSEs. I'd never done them at school because I was always being moved about by the care system. I missed a lot of my education and kept having to settle down and start each course all over again. I was also going to get married. My boyfriend and I had got our own flat and everything. He asked me the other day if I want to get married in here, but I said no. I don't want to remember my wedding being in a prison. I just want to get out.

The system here is well set up for mothers. It's nice staying in the baby unit because I have a single room with Brian and, when he was born, I was given £100 worth of stuff: hats, shawls, cot sheets and so on. I do think we should be allowed to have more visits, like one a week with the baby. At the moment you only get one a fortnight and sometimes the visit only lasts twenty minutes. It's not enough. You're in here, you've got to cope with the baby on your own and you need support. But my baby helps me get through the isolation and loneliness. I look at him and think, 'I've got to get through it for you.'

Sarah

I've been back in prison about four months. I'd only got out of prison a few months before that, after finishing a three-year prison sentence, both in prison and in a young offenders' institute, for GBH and armed robbery. But this is my life, this place. I grew up in the system. Even when I was younger I went through the secure units, the children's homes. My mum couldn't control me, no one could. My dad was murdered when I was three and my brother committed suicide, so I was really messed up. The authorities thought, maybe if they sent me away, I'd calm down. The children's panels said I wasn't allowed to stay at home with my mother because I always got into trouble. But I think all the homes and institutions made me worse. I was deeply disturbed.

I ended up committing manslaughter. I'm guilty and I'm pleading guilty. My brief says I'll probably get a life sentence, or I'll be sectioned and committed to a psychiatric hospital. My psychiatrist says I'm a psychotic schizophrenic. So I'm looking at anything from ten years to life, but a life is a life. I took someone's else's, so now I've got to give up mine.

The guy lived in the basement flat two floors beneath me. I was selling him drugs and he just switched on me. He put on this pornographic video of kids and it made me go crazy. He knew I didn't like people messing around with kids. Even smacking a child. It gets to me. No kid deserves it. And then he tried to touch me up, his hand went round my throat and he started telling me he'd kill me. I think he'd smoked too much crack, but I just went mad at him. I was high on drugs, too, and what made things worse was that I'd been raped two weeks before and had sworn I'd never let a man touch me again. So, when this neighbour started on me, I went mad. I took a knife from his kitchen and I stabbed him.

In a way, it was self-defence, but no one else looks at it like that. I just left him there and went about my business, got on with my life. I didn't tell my boyfriend because he would have beaten me up. For a week I knew the man was down there and I didn't tell anyone. I don't know why.

I was upstairs in the building when the police came round. They kicked his window in. I knew he'd be found. I even sat and made the forensic guys cups of tea and everything. I can't really explain my actions, but I think it was all part of my illness. I know I wouldn't have stabbed the man if he hadn't provoked me but I probably would have beaten him up. I've attacked so many people. I just get into a rage and want to beat people up. Even if they've not done nothing to me. That's why I've been seeing a psychiatrist. I've got a lot of problems.

My psychiatrist told me that I have a split personality, so maybe that's why I don't think about it when I get violent. I don't know. But I'm just not myself when I'm like that. It's quite frightening. I need some therapy, some help, and then, maybe one day, I'll be all right.

I am given drugs: Largactyl, Kemadrin, Welldorm, Tegritol and Anaphrinil, to slow my body down. The doctor keeps putting my medication up. I take 11 tablets a day and 250 mils of the Largactyl in liquid form because its stronger that way. I don't like the medication being put up. I have to take it three times a day.

Before I came here I was on heroin and crack. Not now. I've been in detox and I'm clean. I was on heroin and crack when I killed that guy and I'd been on them since I was fourteen. But I was in trouble long before that.

The first crime I committed was when I was nine. I beat up a twelve-year-old girl and got nicked for it. You know, picked up by the police and locked in a cell until my mother came to get me. It was the first time I'd ever been in a police station. The police cautioned me for what I'd done.

And then another time, a few years later, I got caught shoplifting. My friend was showing me how to shoplift but I couldn't do it. I used to steal something, get it out of the shop, and then take it back in. When I got caught, the police took me to the police station and kept me there all weekend. My mum refused to come and get me out. I was crying, it was horrible.

After being picked up, I started to rebel even more. Against everyone. I started beating people up for nothing. I was sent to a shrink because I was going crazy, hearing voices in my head. In the end I was sent to hospital and I got better for a while.

I think I was fourteen when I first committed armed robbery. Me and a friend were trying to rob this guy and he started screaming at me. He knew me (he lived down the street from me and my friend), but he didn't report us because he knew that we knew all about the stuff he was up to – things he wouldn't want the police to know either.

Everyone used to be frightened of me. I think you can't let yourself get frightened – it only weakens you. I'm a strong person, physically and emotionally, but I'm too strong-headed. I try not to let anything depress me, but sometimes the feelings I get really drag me down, because they make me lose control. When I get like that, I start jumping about. Nobody can speak to me. I bite their head off or I just clump them. I don't want to feel like that. The other day, I broke down crying because I had this overwhelming feeling that I wanted to punch someone. I don't know why. I just broke down crying. I called one of the prison guards and asked them to lock me in my room. I've been asking them to do this nearly every night now. That way, I can't hurt somebody else. If anyone gets hurt, it's me.

My boyfriend comes to see me here but he doesn't know what to say. He just sits and looks at me. He doesn't want me to plead guilty but I've got to. I feel you've got to own up to the things you do – it only makes it worse if you run away.

My boyfriend lives in the flat we bought together. I got some money when my dad and grandma died, then my boyfriend put up half the money for the flat.

My dad was murdered when I was about three. The man who killed him should be out on parole next year. He beat my father with rocks. All because he fancied my mother and he knew he couldn't get her while my dad was there. When I think about what he did to my dad, it makes me want to explode. My little brother couldn't take it any more – he killed himself when he was only fifteen. I really loved him.

Mum's still alive. She's fifty-seven, bless her. She tries her best. I love her but I don't always like her. I don't resent her for sending me to a psychiatrist, because she was only trying to help and, even now, she says she won't give up on me. I'm like her in a lot of ways. She's stubborn, hot-headed and she's always right. She's *always* right. That's why sometimes I don't like her.

I've got four sisters and five brothers – two from my dad, three from the next man, and the other four from the man after that. Mum's been married about five times. But I don't want any kids myself. It would be a sin to bring them into this world – it's so horrible and everyone's at war with each other. There's no peace anywhere.

★

I don't really like the other people here. Some of them are disgusting: bashing things at windows, screaming, giving officers abuse and just acting like animals. They can't even look after themselves. But most of them are just kids, and I can't hate them because I've got to live with them. I mean, I've got to get on with them, it makes my life a lot easier.

In general I don't like women very much. The only ones I speak to are the ones who buy drugs off me. Outside of here, I have no female friends. It's all men. But I do speak to a few of the women here. The girl living next to me – she's lovely, a real diamond. She's about thirty. The other one annoys me sometimes. She gets jealous when I'm talking to other people. She's thirty three. Then there's this other woman who's kind of an authority in here. She's like a mother to me. She always picks me up when I'm down. She's like a rock. From the first moment I came here, she's been my friend.

Prison doesn't stop you committing crimes – it just teaches you new ones. Someone here told me all about 'drumming' – that's burglary. She drums rich people's houses filled with antiques. That's the sort of thing you learn in prison.

But to be honest I quite like it here. I've got security and it makes me feel safe. I will be glad to be leaving this particular prison, though, because I'm moving to a psychiatric hospital at the end of this month. I'll be able to get the help I need there. The psychiatrists here are useless. They ask you how you are feeling and then they don't listen. They write down things you never said.

But I am frightened about the sentence. I don't know why. I want to get the psychiatric help I need, but I'm scared that, if it's a long sentence, I won't be with my mum, and she might die while I'm still locked away.

Viv

My name is Viv and I have been on the streets since I was fourteen, so it has been five years now. My father is Irish. When I was fourteen, I came home from school one day to find a note on the door, saying he'd gone back to Ireland. So that was it. My mother had died when I was twelve, and we lived in a council flat, so I couldn't stay there on my own.

When my mum died, I went a bit mad. I started bullying other kids in school, taking their dinner money off them, waiting for them at the school gates and beating them up round the corner. I even got caught smoking crack-cocaine in the toilet. Then I beat up three kids just outside the school, so the teachers found out. Eventually I got expelled and had to go to a different place. Despite all of that I enjoyed myself in school. I think it was the best time of my life.

The decision to live on the streets was a difficult one. I could have gone into care or something like that but I didn't want to. I've always looked after myself. But that didn't stop me being frightened. I was only fourteen, everybody else was a lot older than me, and I didn't know anyone. I was really scared and it took me about three months to get used to it. Even now, after five years, I still get frightened sometimes, like when I am on my own late at night.

I have been a heroin addict, I've been a crack addict, but now I'm clean. I started getting into solvents at one point – lighter gas and stuff – but I'm off that, too. All I do is smoke a joint now and again and that's just an occasional thing. Apart from that, I've done really well.

I have been attacked on the streets, when I was younger, but that hasn't happened since I was sixteen. People round here know that I can look after myself, so nobody really starts at me anymore. Things are a lot easier than they were at first.

When I first came to the streets, I went where most people go – the Strand, in London. That's what got me into drugs and stuff, because I met a lot of alcoholics and addicts there. Now I just keep away from them all. I mean, I have got friends – well, acquaintances – who are addicts but I keep my distance. I can't go near the Strand now, anyway, because I kicked somebody in the throat and he went straight through Boots the Chemist's window. I went to prison for that and there's an injunction stopping me entering the street.

It would all be new faces there, anyway, compared to when I first came here. People change all the time and they move on – apart from a few alcoholics who have been around for fifteen to twenty years. The advantage of the Strand is that you get all the soup runs, so you are well fed.

A lot of people can't handle life on the streets and they only last about three to six months. A lot of them are a total waste of time. But you can make friends, too. Matt is my street brother. A street brother is somebody you look after and who looks after you. Matt is sixteen years old and he's great. We get on really well, although sometimes he can be a bit of a pain. If I've got some money I try to help Matt out and I know he'd do the same for me. He is on gear, but he tries to stay away from it.

I normally sleep in the daytime so I am awake at night, because the West End is a really noisy place at night. You'd expect it to be the other way round, but it is quieter during the day. At night, I tend to go begging. Begging used to be good, you used to be able to make some decent money, but now it's a waste of time because there are too many people doing it. People think they can make money down here so they come to London to try it out. That means it's pretty pointless begging any more, but it's still a way of trying to get some money.

The thing that annoys me about street-life is there are too many idiots around here. They just muck everything up. There used to be places where you could go and get free cakes and so on, but then you had people coming along and getting stuff for four or five people and the shop owners just got fed up. Homeless people are banned from McDonald's now, because of some idiots who got caught drinking, fighting and taking drugs in the toilets. That's what it's like. Some people just mucking it up for everyone else.

Being homeless depends on the person you are and how you cope with the experience. I get along with everybody, I talk to anyone but, if they start taking liberties, that's the end of it. I've had fights in the street. I've got a scar on my arm where I got stabbed and I've had a scaffolding bar across my kneecap. I've had quite a few bad fights, but now people leave me alone. Some people can't cope with it all. I have seen so many people come to the streets and end up dead. A few of my acquaintances – good acquaintances – have killed themselves because they couldn't handle it. I'm not immune to the depression it causes, either, and I've been tempted by suicide more than once. I suffer from manic depression because of all the drugs and everything else I've been through, and I've got scars on my arms where I self-harmed.

At one point I had a flat in Peckham, on the North Peckham Estate. It's one of the worst estates in London, and I got broken into four times in six months. In the end I went to the council and said, 'You can keep your flat!' Now I'm on a council waiting list and I've been promised a new flat in a different area in November.

Life on the streets can be difficult, and I've had my fair share of trouble, but it also has its lighter moments. I am a bit of a comedian and I make everybody laugh. Last night, for example, there were all these football supporters from Sunderland. They were miserable because their team had lost but I was still able to make them laugh. I could make people laugh twenty-four hours a day, seven days a week. It's nice to be like that, it makes me feel good.

Hanna

It was during a visit to Ireland that I first came into contact with drugs. I was sixteen. I took part in a student exchange between Frankfurt, my home town in Germany, and Dublin. I fell in love with Ireland, with all the people I met, with the language and the culture. I was amazed by the kindness of everyone, and the easy-going lifestyle, which is completely different from Germany.

Liz, my student exchange, and I got on really well with each other and we became very close friends.

On the first Saturday night, we went with some of Liz's friends to a disco in a small neighbouring town. Before going to the disco, everyone met in a pub to get in the 'mood'. Soon, I realised what the 'mood' was. Liz and her friends consumed loads of beer, whiskey and hash. Every five minutes a joint was passed around and I was always offered a drag of it. I was a little bit shocked, and I said no every time, because I had never seen people taking drugs before and I didn't expect them to be so obvious about it.

Because I had never been exposed to drugs, I had all these prejudiced ideas about what sort of people take them. I thought that someone who took drugs would be on the dole, not very well educated, with a childhood full of problems. But the people I saw smoking drugs were healthy, normal young people just like me.

The following weekend, I didn't say no when the joint was passed my way. I drank as much as Liz and I smoked as much hash as she did. She and her friends didn't force me to, it was my own decision. I wanted to know how it felt. Well, I didn't feel anything physical, maybe because it was the first time. But I did feel something else; I became a part of them, a part of the unity the Irish are when they are sharing something.

The next time I was in Ireland was a year later. Liz and I were going to a party with a group of her friends and Liz asked me what I would say if she took an E that night. I remember it very clearly, because the first thing that came into my mind was my first joint a year earlier. I'd joined in on that occasion but I hoped no one expected me to do this as well. I told Liz I didn't mind as long as she didn't change her character and freak out. I needn't have worried because, throughout the party, she seemed perfectly normal.

But that night I noticed that everything had changed since my first visit. Liz's best friends were all on drugs – not only on the night of the party but every day. A few of them consumed more than they could afford, so they were buying on credit and, as everyone knows, that's not a good idea.

However, it didn't stop me from wanting to visit Liz and her friends in Ireland and over the past two years I have spent a great deal of my time there. One thing it has made me realise, though, is how quickly people can change, how they can become someone completely different. The experiences of Liz and most of her friends were nothing compared to what happened to another mutual friend, Mary.

I met Mary through Liz. They went to college together. Mary was eighteen when she took her first hit of cocaine. She was not a very strong person so it was not long before she began to cut herself off from Liz and hang around with another gang. Six months later, she broke completely with her old friends and spent all her time selling drugs for a dealer so that she could earn money to support her habit. By this time she wasn't on cocaine or speed or LSD anymore – she was addicted to heroin.

To get the money for her shots, she didn't just stick to dealing; she also started stealing everything she saw. She broke into houses, stole bikes, anything she could lay her hands on. Mary must have been desperate. She tried to commit suicide a few times but she was always found in time to be rescued. She didn't have the strength to break out of the vicious circle drugs create and she always went back to the needle.

A few months later, she got pregnant and, by the time she realised she was pregnant, it was too late for an abortion. But she never did have the child. The baby couldn't deal with the poisonous drugs in Mary's system and she lost it. It sounds cruel, but in a way I think that losing the baby was probably for the best, given Mary's situation.

Mary's parents were always on her side. Although their daughter had changed so much, they still tried to help her. At one stage, when Mary was really down, she realised that she would never make it on her own, so her parents offered to organise some therapy for her. I think she accepted and I guess that is where she is now – in therapy or rehabilitation.

It takes time to leave behind you the stuff that makes you forget who you are. I hope that one day Mary will lead a normal life again, but I know that giving up drugs is a battle and no one can make it on their own. Addicts need their family and their friends. We all have to give them the feeling that they are not alone, that they are still wanted and that their life is worth living. The problem is that most of us are ignorant, narrow-minded creatures. We don't see that people with a serious drug problem or alcoholics or criminals are what we are – human beings. They deserve our help and support in every way.

Earlier this year, I returned to Ireland for a short visit with my boyfriend and I noticed that Liz and the others never mention Mary any more. I hope that what happened to her will make them realise that drugs are not harmless toys.

Joanne

I'm in Holloway prison for importing cocaine into Britain. I've been here since last October, which is almost a year now. I'm waiting to be sentenced. I was found guilty, but I'm not. This is what happened.

I used to live in Jamaica with my grandmother. She was very sick with a weak heart and diabetes. I went to live in England but decided I wanted to visit her and the rest of my family. My parents split up when I was six and that was a very painful period of my life. My dad now lives with his girlfriend and my mum lives in a totally different place.

So, while I was visiting my grandmother, I met this guy, Patrick, in a nightclub. He came up to me and said, 'I haven't seen you here before.' I told him that was because I was living in England but I had a Jamaican passport. I was very young and was really impressed by him. He was thirty-four, very caring, and he had lots of money. He said he had his own business, an off-licence, and he owned a brand new Honda Accord and a Toyota jeep. I started seeing him about three times a week and he even used to come to my house to talk to my grandmother. I really loved him and never thought he would be into anything dodgy – he looked like a business type.

When it was time for me to return to England to continue my studies, Patrick lent me two suitcases. He said he had borrowed them from a friend in Wolverhampton the last time he was over and asked if I could deliver them back to her on my way home to Staffordshire. He gave me her address and telephone number and I kept the information in my filofax. What I didn't know was that both the cases contained cocaine.

Patrick came with me to Kingston airport and, while I was waiting to board the plane to London, we bumped into some friends of his. At the time, I thought this was just a coincidence. One of the friends, Carl, was catching the same flight as me but we didn't sit together on the plane.

I was arrested when we landed at Gatwick. I was searched and then detained for a day. I was only eighteen. There were three and a half kilos of cocaine in the cases. I didn't notice that they were particularly heavy because I'd never used Samsonite cases before. In Jamaica, we don't have Samsonite. The cocaine was in a false compartment. They just looked like normal suitcases to me. One had my food and presents for my school friends and the other, the bigger one, had my clothes. Customs discovered cocaine in both of them.

Carl, Patrick's friend, was standing in a different queue

from me because he's British Jamaican and carries a British passport (mine has a visa for Britain, saying 'Indefinite stay'). He was also stopped. But he said he didn't know anything about me and the smuggling, and customs were satisfied with the statement he gave them. He was only detained for three minutes and then he left.

I said to the customs, 'I don't know what you are talking about. You've got the wrong person. I don't know anything about cocaine. I've never even seen it before.' When we landed at Gatwick, I'd left the suitcases unattended while I went to the toilet and bought a phonecard. If I'd known they were full of drugs, I wouldn't have left them lying around the airport, would I?

I told the police all about Patrick and the girl in Wolverhampton. They asked me if I knew what this girl looked like but all that Patrick had told me was that she had dreadlocks. I gave them the telephone number from my filofax but she had changed it. Eventually they tracked her down through a mobile number she was ringing from in Wolverhampton. She was taken to court but she said the suitcases were not hers, so they let her go. As she was leaving the court, she flashed me a couple of dirty looks, as if to say, 'You've grassed.' I think she and Patrick must have expected me to keep my mouth shut.

The police also had a video of Carl putting my cases onto a trolley at the airport, but Carl disappeared back to Jamaica a week before my trial and, anyway, he'd already said he didn't know anything about me. Of course, when I tried to phone Patrick, he'd changed his number.

★

My barrister did her best. I told the police and the court everything, but they still found me guilty. Probation came to see me recently for a pre-sentence report so that the judge can read about me. Now I just have to wait for sentencing.

I'm really depressed because my solicitor has told me that, for the amount of cocaine I was carrying, I am looking at at least ten years in prison. If that is what I get, I will serve half of it here in a British prison and then I will be deported back to Jamaica for the second half. I don't know if the Jamaican police will make me finish my sentence but it doesn't matter — even after the first five years, my youth will be finished. And I can't do it. I can't serve five years in prison. I just can't face it.

My only hope at the moment is that my barrister had a trainee with her in court who overheard three of the jury discussing my case at a train station. They are not supposed to talk about cases together outside the court, so my barrister mentioned it to the judge. I don't know what's going to happen, but I'm hoping for a retrial.

My family are not taking this very well. My mum has been in hospital with high blood pressure. I write to her and phone sometimes. My auntie is the only one living here in Britain. I thought she would be supportive because I am only young and in prison so I wrote to her and said, 'I'm in bigger trouble than I thought and I need a shoulder to cry on.' But she wrote back saying, 'Our shoulders are already heavy with the shame.' My uncle worked with the Jamaican prime minister, and that is why my auntie feels that I have disgraced the family. But I've never been in trouble with the police before. I don't smoke or drink, or take dope.

I think I've been used. I don't know if the whole thing was a set-up but I do know that I never want to see Patrick again. If he was interested in me, if he cared for me at all, then he would be looking after me now. But he's not. He's changed his telephone number and I can't reach him. He hasn't tried to contact me, either.

I think he chooses people who the police are unlikely to suspect. Me, for example. When I met him I was only eighteen years old and I looked very innocent. Too innocent to be trafficking drugs. The police are certainly aware of him. They found his name and number in the filofax of another girl who is in here for drug smuggling, so they know he exists. She is in here for organising the smuggling, so it must be some kind of ring.

If Patrick had said, 'I'm offering you an opportunity to earn a nice sum of money if you smuggle for me,' I wouldn't have accepted. I was comfortable as I was – I wanted to be a nursery nurse and I was supposed to start college in September. I would have stayed and worked in England, gained some experience and then gone home.

Instead, I have just spent my nineteenth birthday in prison. I knew importation carried very heavy sentences. I knew the consequences, so why would I do it?

There are loads of other girls in here for the same thing. Some were set up, but a lot knew what they were doing. Sometimes the ones who are guilty go free. I know one girl who got away with it because she swallowed the cocaine, but it wasn't as much as three and a half kilos. Mine was worth half a million pounds.

Up north in England, where I lived, we didn't have a big drug problem. I don't think kids should be dealing drugs.

I feel very alone here but I don't trust any of the other prisoners. They want to know all your business, then gossip about you to everyone else. I just go to the chapel on Sundays and that's about it.

When I am sentenced I will be shipped out of Holloway because I'm a young offender and young people here are only on remand. I think I will probably be sent to Bulwood Hall. But prison is prison. What difference does it make where you are?

I'm just blocking my mind, not thinking about the future. I am so depressed I've even thought about killing myself, but when I mention it to people they say I'm just being silly. I wouldn't wish my experience on anyone. It's something that has affected my entire life – my family, my friends and my education – and it is something I'll always carry with me.

Sylvia

I'm nineteen and I'm from Trinidad. Things were not going so well for me in England, I was lonely, and I wanted to go back home. But I had one major problem and that is what got me into trouble. Basically, I obtained a property by deception. A birth certificate. A false one.

I first came over to England when I was quite young, about fifteen. My mum and dad were going through a massive divorce – they'd been together for twenty-two years – and I was having a hard time coping with the situation. I didn't really understand what was going on and nobody explained it to me. We were living in Trinidad at the time. Then my cousin arrived on a visit and she said that she was willing to bring me back to England with her. She said that she would take care of me. It seemed like the perfect solution.

My cousin had applied for a council house near Crawley and was staying in a hostel until it was sorted out. So in the meantime I stayed with a woman she knew up in Leeds. I lived there for quite a while because, when my cousin actually got the house, she said I should wait until it was ready – she had to paint it and everything. The woman in Leeds said, 'Okay, no problem.' She understood my situation. I was so grateful to her that I kept in contact with her and wrote her letters after I moved out.

Although I felt very homesick, I tried to make the best of things. I missed my family and my friends and I really wanted to go back home, but I thought, 'Well, this is an opportunity for me,' and I was determined to make the most of it. So, I went to college and I did quite well.

Then one day, about a year later, I came home from college to find all my things dumped outside the flat with a note from my cousin. It said, 'I'm sorry to do this but I have to get on with my life as well and I'm too young to have such a responsibility.' My cousin was about twenty-four at the time.

I couldn't believe it. I'd done nothing to upset her. I was really quiet around the house and just got on with things. I didn't know what to do. I just sat there.

At that time, I was doing a paper-round to get money for my bus pass and so on. The newsagent I worked for had a kind of shack to store things in and that's where I stayed, without anybody knowing, even though it was winter. The shack was very, very small, about the size of a table and, of course, it had no washing facilities so I had to go to the washroom in McDonald's. That's how I got by for the next fortnight. It was quite short, but painful.

During that time I saved up my earnings from the newspaper round and when I had enough I bought a bus pass and travelled to Bromley. I didn't know why I was going there. I just travelled. In Bromley I started looking for somewhere to go to the bathroom. I had a sack with some clothes and a toothbrush in it and I wanted to fix myself up. I ended up in the washroom of Bromley Hospital, which was lucky, because I spotted a notice there about some job vacancies.

I had qualifications because I'd been going to college for a year and had passed all my GCSEs. The job I applied for was as a care assistant. In the interview, they asked me where I lived and I gave them the old address, at my cousin's house. I got the job. I had a choice about how many hours to do and I told them I just wanted three hours a day, because I still had college.

So I had a job, but still had nowhere to live. My hours at the hospital were from five to eight in the evening and when everybody went home, I stayed upstairs in one of the changing rooms.

About two weeks later I saw an ad in the window of the same newsagents I'd worked in before: 'To Let'. I didn't understand what To Let meant at first. I thought it was TOILET with the 'i' missing! But it was an advert for a room in a house and that's where I stayed for over two years.

My job paid me about £130 a fortnight. My rent was £50 a week so I had about £15 a week to live on. For food, I just bought bread – you know, the most important things. Sometimes, when I had the chance, I'd do extra time to earn more money and, if I had any left at the end of the week, it went straight into my bank account. When I first came over, my cousin had made sure that I had a bank account. At least she did that much.

I continued at college and got my geography, art and maths A levels. By this time my sister was living in the area and I moved in with her. But when college was finished, I started to feel really fed up and just wanted to go back home again to Trinidad. It was then that I realised I had a problem.

It had been two years since my cousin threw me out and I had had no word from her. She still had my passport with my birth certificate and I thought that I couldn't get back to Trinidad without them. I tried her old address but she wasn't there. She could have been anywhere for all I knew.

I contacted my parents but I didn't tell them about the passport. My aunt has a friend who gets air tickets cheap, so she offered to pay for my fare back home. I was desperate.

My first plan was to go to the airport and give myself up to the deportee section but when I thought about this, I was scared about what might happen and how long I would have to stay there. I thought that maybe I would have to go to jail when I got home. But my entry into England was legal so there should have been some record. I didn't know what to do. I just did not have a *clue* how to go about finding records or copies of my papers. I didn't understand the system and I still don't. I had no

98

one to help me, no support or guidance. All I kept thinking was, how do I get home?

So, for two days, I sat on my bed trying to come up with a plan and what I came up with was a name, Lydia Gaynor. I don't know any 'Lydia's' and I only know one 'Gaynor' but what I wanted was a sweet name that I could go under. A sweet, innocent name that could pass for me.

My sister knew what I was trying to do, but she had no part in it. I went to the register of births and deaths and looked to see if there was anyone by that name. I was lucky – there was one Lydia Gaynor who was only two years younger than me. When I looked her up in the register, it gave me everything I needed to get a false birth certificate. It only took me about an hour and a half and there I was with a new identity. Ready and willing to go. I called my aunt and asked her to put the air ticket in the name of Lydia Gaynor. She didn't ask why.

The next step was to get a passport. Well, the first thing they asked at the passport office was, 'Where's your mum?' Because I – 'Lydia Gaynor' – was only seventeen years old and I had said that my address was the old one I had in Leeds. So I said my mum worked in shifts and it was quite hard for her to come down to London with me.

I thought everything had gone smoothly and it wasn't long before the passport office called me back and told me that my passport was ready for collection. But, when I went to get it, one of the officials called me into this room and, before I could say anything, these two big hefty men in uniform appeared. All I could do was cry because I was in a state of shock. That was three weeks ago.

I know what I did was wrong, but I want people to understand why I did it, because there is always a reason why people do what they do. I know I'm guilty; I know I had no right to take someone else's identity.

After I was arrested, the police took me to a police station in Peterborough. I had to sit on this chair, while they took my photos, and did my fingerprints. Then I was interviewed. I gave them my name and told them everything but because they caught me with a birth certificate in somebody else's name and I had no ID of my own, they weren't sure if I was telling them the truth. I spent the night in the police station while they tried to find evidence.

Then, the following day, they took me to court, where I explained everything to my solicitor: my background, living on the streets, everything. The solicitor told me that there is a Trinidad Embassy, where they could look for my file, find out where I was born and get me a replacement passport. I wish I'd known about that earlier.

I've been in jail for three weeks now. Convicted, on remand, it's the same thing. The reason they are holding me is that they still don't have any evidence about who I really am. The night I was arrested, I gave them my sister's telephone number but I have no idea where she's disappeared to. I don't know if she's gone mad or something since this happened, but she's just not there anymore.

So, every Friday, I have to go to court and they keep asking me who I really am; who is Lydia Gaynor? And what am I doing with her birth certificate? I suppose they think there might be a more serious story behind the one I'm telling.

My solicitor thinks that I only have three more weeks to go because the most I can get for having a false birth certificate is three months, and you usually only do half of what you get. The first thing I'm going to do when I get out is contact the Trinidad Embassy, get my papers and go home. What I am scared of is that they will keep me in this prison until they find my file at the embassy which could take months.

I'm worried about my mum because she knew I was on my way back. The flight my aunt bought me was an open ticket but Mum must have been expecting me by now. She doesn't know that I'm in prison. She is really soft and I don't want to upset her. This would break her heart.

Some of the people here are all right, others scare me, but at the end of the day, I just try to laugh as much as I can. I have learnt my lesson now and, if I don't laugh, I know I will be depressed. When I first came in, I was so depressed I could not eat for a week and I was really ill.

So I try to look on the positive side. I know that I am lucky. I will be leaving here soon, but there are other girls who will be in prison for years. I am shocked by the lives of some of them. Still, if you commit the crime, you have to do the time and I've learnt a lot during my time in here. We take life for granted, you know. All the simple things that we think are nothing really are something, and you don't realise that until those things have gone. When I leave here I won't take anything, or anyone, for granted. I think I will look at people in a different way. You never understand another person's situation until you experience it yourself. The minute I walk out those gates, I will never be the same again.

Vida

I'm seventeen and at the moment I am working, selling advertising space, because I decided to move out of home. I couldn't support myself doing my A levels, so I am going to work this year and then go back into education next year. I moved out because I wasn't getting on with my mum and, anyway, it was the right time to leave. To cut the cord.

I've been involved in political action since I was thirteen. I'd always been brought up anti-nuclear and fairly liberal left-wing. My grandparents took my mother and aunt on Aldermaston Marches in the fifties. But I first became directly involved through my brother. He's a freelance journalist and about four years ago he wrote an article about landmines. CND called him up to comment on the issue and I was the one who answered the phone.

I knew a bit about the nuclear debate because I'd read a book called *Goggle Eyes* by Anne Fine, which talked about anti-nuclear activities in the eighties. At the time

I'd vaguely thought about getting involved but hadn't really bothered to find out more. So, when CND called to speak to my brother, it was the perfect opportunity. They passed my name on to the CND youth department, who got in touch.

The first thing I did was in Trafalgar Square on 29 October 1994, when CND had a big rally. I went down to the youth office the day before the rally to help get things organised, printing leaflets and generally getting ready for the demo.

After that I used to go to the offices every week to help out – stuffing envelopes and things – but it wasn't particularly interesting. I think Youth CND was in a bit of a crisis at the time because it didn't have all that many volunteers.

In April of the next year, however, things became more lively, when Youth CND organised the first Aldermaston March since the seventies or eighties. It was Youth CND only, and we had a wicked time, even though there were only about twenty-five of us.

The march took us four days. We set the whole thing up – the route and stopping points were all pre-arranged. We slept in church halls and community centres that had been organised in advance. The march finished up in London and, when we got there, there were a couple of thousand people waiting for us, organised by CND, for our welcome. There were police around – there always are at these things – but there were no arrests, no trouble. It was brilliant.

I was the youngest on the march, still only thirteen. The next youngest was seventeen. But everyone accepted me as an equal. In fact, ever since I've been involved in politics, I have never been patronised or looked down on by other campaigners, which is brilliant. I suppose people who are politically aware couldn't justify being patronising to someone purely because of their age. If everyone deserves an equal chance, regardless of sex or class or colour, then age surely also applies.

In 1995 Chirac, the president of France then, announced that he was going to do nuclear tests, so we decided to have regular Tuesday night protest parties outside the French Embassy. It was a formal vigil but with a lot of loud and colourful music, drums, very much in your face. Straight after the first of these I went to Glastonbury for the first time. CND do a lot of campaigning work at the festival – leafleting and fundraising.

I was more or less involved in continuous campaigning by this stage but the next big event was in August of that year – the fiftieth anniversary of the dropping of bombs on Hiroshima and Nagasaki. There was huge action planned for 9 August (the anniversary of Nagasaki) at Faslane in Scotland, which is where British Trident nuclear submarines are stored. Direct action was planned, that is *action*, rather than simply a rally or protest. What we planned to do was march from our peace camp to the base and block the base all day. It was at this protest that I first got arrested.

★

It was a really hot August day. We all marched to the north gate and did a 'Die-In' there – at exactly the point when the bomb was dropped on Nagasaki (I think it was 11.02 a.m.), everyone screams and drops to the floor. There are smoke bombs, too. It's highly effective, very dramatic and, for those involved, a symbolic moment. Afterwards we blockaded that gate for a while, then a group of people went off to the south gate with the intention of blockading that one, too. We went with them but then a few of us decided to return to the north gate. When we arrived a car was coming out. So, we jumped out of our van and sat down in the car's path and linked arms.

It was the quickest lot of arrests I've ever seen. The police just piled in and, one by one, they managed to unlink our arms and drag us apart until I was the only one left sitting there in front of the car, which was revving its engine at me. I was thinking: Oh my God! What am I doing? How did I end up in this position? I wasn't bothered by the police, just the car! The driver was looking really angry.

I needn't have worried – it wasn't long before they arrested me, too. The police separated us out and chucked us into two vans, women in one and men in another. I got put in the women's van first and was joined by a friend of mine, who had been dragged along the floor. All the skin was grazed and bleeding on one leg and she was quite distraught. Her leg was a complete mess. Another friend of mine had been 'quick-cuffed'. These were new handcuffs with teeth on the inside, which can really hurt your hands when they are snapped on. Not all the forces around Britain had them but the Ministry of Defence police were using them at the demo. Quite often with peace arrests, no one gets hurt, but the girl who had been quick-cuffed and I had never been arrested before so it was all a bit of a shock. The three of us sat shaking in the van.

We were taken to a police station in the Glasgow area and I was there for about seven to eight hours. The guy who processed me, who took all my belongings off me and filled in the forms, had a very strong accent and spoke really fast. I had to keep on asking him to repeat himself and he was getting angry. I was trying not to laugh because I was nervous.

As soon as the police found out my age, they separated me from everyone else and put me in a juvenile cell. They didn't charge me – they let me off because they couldn't be bothered to deal with a minor. I was released into the hands of one of the other activists, who was over twenty-one. If they had arrested me it would have been for breach of peace. The Scottish papers covered the demo, saying that forty people were arrested on the anniversary of Nagasaki.

My mother knew what had happened because the police called her from the station. She told me that she had been expecting it to happen. At the time, she didn't mind me being arrested, because it wasn't for something like theft or drugs. It was political and she agreed with anti-nuclear campaigns. But it wasn't a pleasant experience. It was quite scary, especially as I was only thirteen. On the other hand, I knew that if I started to do direct action I would be arrested at some point. In a way, I sort of wanted to get the first arrest over with, because then I would know what to expect. It also gave me more confidence about confronting the police. If you are brought up in a middle-class family, you have a certain awe of, and respect for, the police and it made getting into confrontations with them quite difficult for me. Being arrested really helped to get rid of that attitude and I felt more comfortable about going into action. I never got involved in demos with the intention of getting arrested, but I always knew it might be on the cards.

September 1995 was the Aldershot arms fair. Campaign against the Arms Trade organised a march to the fair and I decided to join them. (Once you're involved with one organisation your name gets passed on to others.) I don't really know what happened but there was some kind of mess-up with the police. It had been agreed that we would be allowed to walk to the gate, then sit down and do our symbolic blockade thing, but if anyone got out of line or tried to run into the base there would be trouble. So, we set off from a car park towards the gate, which was about two hundred metres away. Then, after only about twenty metres, the cops said, 'Right, you're not going any further.' Everyone was stunned. So we started running in all directions, trying to get behind the police line. I was arrested almost straight away for aggravated trespass under the Criminal Justice Act. Aggravated trespass is trespass on private land in the open air. There is no trespass law for buildings, which is quite interesting. Apparently the land we ran on to was private property.

The police were really unpleasant, even though they didn't charge me in the end. They treated me like a juvenile delinquent. I come from a stable background and I was doing what I was doing because I had thought about it rationally and because it was something I believed in. I am not a juvenile delinquent. Being treated like one makes me even more angry with the police.

The next time I got arrested was at Chequers, when Chirac came to talk to John Major about Anglo–French nuclear collaboration. CND had organised a big protest, about two hundred people, and we were all standing around having a vigil. I think whoever was inside didn't give a shit about the vigil and they would barely have been aware of our presence, anyway, because we were too far away. So, a group of us decided to do something more active. The electrified fences were only two feet high; we could step over them and that's exactly what we did.

Carrying our banners, we headed across the fields towards the main buildings. Suddenly, police on horseback began galloping towards us. One of them came charging at me and gathered me up off the ground. It was really scary. I was taken to the closest police station and cautioned. So, I still had no record.

After that, I stopped getting myself arrested for a while. My mum was concerned that it could go further than simply being arrested and that I might end up in prison.

So, for two years, until September 1997, I avoided direct action. If I attended an event where there was direct action, I acted as a legal observer instead. It was very hard to stand back, as I wanted to be doing something effective. On the other hand, I knew that the role of legal observer was important, too.

So, the very last time I got arrested was at the Royal Navy and British Army Equipment Exhibition in Farnborough, a government arms fair. Robin Cook was spouting his 'ethical foreign policy' nonsense and yet at the same time our country was hosting a fair where torture weapons were on sale and countries such as Turkey and Indonesia, whose governments are known for human rights abuses, were guests.

The fair took place the day after Princess Diana's death, so there weren't many people from the press there as the papers were all covering the accident. All the same, the protest was very effective. There was a huge number of peace activists there and they had constructed two enormous blockades. Then several double-decker buses full of people from the Kurdish community arrived, who were all extremely angry. The police were in chaos, so demonstrators were able to get right into the base and walk around, although most of the Kurds stayed outside, as they didn't want hassle from immigration.

A few of us 'found' a hole in the fence and climbed in. We split off into ones and twos, aiming to get right into the exhibition itself. But I was spotted by the police and arrested, again for trespassing. This time they charged me. I signed all the charge sheets, knowing that it would not come to anything because you have to be sixteen to go to a magistrates court and I was only fifteen. They sent me to a juvenile court, but they ended up dropping the case.

I think the police were wary because the year before they had spent about a million pounds trying to get peace activists booked for trespassing at the same fair. The activists had a lawyer who researched the local district and discovered that the land they had 'trespassed' on was, in fact, public property from some ancient law. So, every case was dropped. It cost the authorities a fortune and I don't think they wanted to risk another similar humiliation.

After that, I made a conscious decision to slow things down for a while. I'd spent a lot of time bunking off school to be politically active and it was beginning to affect my work. A lot of people kept telling me I was going to do really badly at school because of this, so I made a conscious effort to do well. I didn't want my politics to be found 'at fault' because of bad results in my GCSEs. But I did really well, so that was okay.

Taking a break from direct action meant that I could concentrate more on political theory. Until the last year and a half, I only had vague ideas about what I believed in and what I didn't. More recently I have made an effort to read up and teach myself about various political beliefs and it has given me a wider understanding of the issues.

So, although for the time being I have stopped direct action, my politics have become more extreme. This is why I am at odds with my mother now. I believe that her politics are middle-class and, because our politics used to be similar, I think she feels I've moved away. Now, if asked to define myself politically or give myself a label, I would say that I am an anarchist. My mother does not like that.

Our views on the police are very different. I have a huge problem with them. I believe they are servers of the state and my contact with them has always been completely unpleasant, therefore I have no respect for them. I don't believe their existence is necessary. Here, my mother disagrees with me. Although she knows that they are not always a good force, she believes they are necessary. I think Mum thinks my beliefs are too extreme for my experiences; I am not black or working-class, therefore I am not oppressed and haven't been persecuted all my life.

I would no longer describe myself as completely non-violent, either. I wouldn't go up to a policeman and randomly punch him in the face. I am not a violent person, but I am much more prepared to defend myself and the political ideas I stand for. I wouldn't stand by and watch someone harming an individual because of the principle of non-violence, so why should I let organisations or governments destroy the planet and the people on it? They deserve to be defended. But governments and multinationals have a lot of power and money, and I don't think we can live by principles of non-violence alone, and be successful in our aims. I won't initiate violence but I won't stand by and watch the world get completely trashed and people get killed needlessly in the name of profit. I won't allow it to happen.

Contributors' Notes

Amy is now twenty-two. She has been working for the police force in north London since she was eighteen.

Angela was born and brought up in Wales. Recently she met up with an old friend and moved to England with him where she is now very happy.

Carol is fifteen and lives with her mother, her younger sister and her cat. She goes to an all-girls school and is about to enter Year Ten. She loves swimming and goes whenever she can. When she leaves school, she would like to go into design and to travel. Her favourite subjects are design, technology, textiles and English.

Catherine is nineteen. Before going to prison, she was hoping to train as a solicitor.

Debbie is now twenty-two. She has been working as a prostitute on the streets for several years, to support her heroin habit. She has a baby daughter with foster parents.

Ella is eighteen. She is in prison on remand, awaiting trial for shoplifting. Her daughter, who was born when Ella was fourteen, is in foster care. What she dreams of is a happy family life – the chance to begin again.

Emily is eighteen. She has just left school and started a foundation course at a well-established art school. She lives in a student house with seven others.

Hanna is twenty years old. She has now returned home to live and work in an insurance office in Frankfurt. She is engaged to a young German who is living and working in a television distribution company in Paris. She wrote her piece in English, though German is her mother tongue.

Joanne's hobbies include dancing but, at the moment, all she dreams of is getting out of prison and going back to Jamaica. One day she would like to have a family of her own there.

Lara is eighteen. Whilst in prison, she gave birth to a son. She maintains her innocence and wants to go home and bring up her son in peace.

Sarah has recently turned nineteen. While in prison, Sarah discovered that she takes great pleasure in gardening. She also enjoys art therapy.

Sweet Pea is studying at the moment and using her time in prison to do her A levels. She has also been learning to cook. She has begun to make some more friends in prison but remains very lonely.

Sylvia is nineteen. She dreams of swimming in the Trinidadian sea again and being back with her aunt and family. Her ambition is to write a book and she would like to include an account of this incident in it.

Tara is in her early twenties. She has a small, terraced house on the outskirts of greater London. She lives on benefit, has two children and does voluntary work.

Vida is seventeen. She is living with her dad while she saves enough money to get a flat and then go travelling. She has taken a year out of school to work and give herself independence. She is a peace activist and enjoys campaigning.

Viv is living on the streets. She is nineteen and is waiting to be housed by the council. She loves music and playing the fool and her ideal job would be one in which she could make people laugh.

Resources

General

Brook
Free confidential advice about sex and contraception for under–25s.
Call free: 0800 018 5023

ChildLine
For children and young people in trouble or danger.
Call free: 0800 1111

Samaritans
If you are in crisis and need to talk to someone. 24 hours a day for the cost of a local call.
Tel: 0345 909090/02476 678678

THOMAS Organisation
This organisation helps anyone who is on the margins of

society; excluded or living on the edge. They help young people rebuild their lives after drugs, prison, leaving home and family crises.
St Anne's House, France Street, Blackburn, BB2 1LX
Tel: 01254 59240

YWCA
Gives advice and information on a broad range of issues from drug abuse to counselling to violence.
Tel: 01865 304 200

Abuse and Violence

Butterflies Support Group
For young women who have experienced childhood abuse. Manchester area.
Tel: 0161 794 0837

42nd Street
Group and individual counselling for young women aged 14–25 in the Manchester, Salford and Trafford area who have experienced sexual violence or are under stress.
Fourth Floor, Swan Buildings, 20 Swan Street, Manchester, M4 5JW
Tel: 0161 832 0170

Young Women's Project, Dundee Rape Crisis Centre
Free and confidential service offering advice and support for young women who have been abused at any time.

Helpline: Thursdays 6–8 p.m. Reversed charge calls accepted.
PO Box 83, Dundee, DD1 9PF
Tel: 01382 206222
Fax: 01382 201291

see also ChildLine and Samaritans above

Drugs and Alcohol

Alcohol Concern
Advice and information for people concerned about their drinking or the drinking of those close to them. Puts you in contact with their nearest agency.
Tel: 020 7928 7377

Cocaine Anonymous
A helpline for users of cocaine.
Tel: 020 7284 3031

Detox Five
A five day opiate detox programme.
Tel: 0800 515 282

Narcotics Anonymous
Helps people who have a drug addiction.
Suite 6, 38 Ebury Street, Victoria, London, SW1W OLU
Tel: 020 7730 0009

National Drugs Helpline

Gives advice about coping with drugs.
Tel: 0800 776600

Family Support Groups

The Bourne Trust

This organisation has served and supported prisoners and their families for over a hundred years.
Lincoln House, 1-3 Brixton Road, London SW9 6DE
Tel: 020 7582 1313
Fax: 020 7735 6077

POPS

Partners of Prisoners is a family support group serving north England and Wales. It gives advice to families and friends of prisoners on visiting rights, arranging prison moves, deportation, accommodation and legal issues.
St Mark's Cheetham, Tetlow Lane, Cheetham, Manchester, M8 9HF
Tel: 0161 740 8600
Fax: 0161 740 4181

Women in Prison

A support and campaigning organisation for women prisoners. Visits prisons and provides practical advice on welfare issues.
3b Aberdeen Studios, 22 Highbury Gardens, London, N5 2EA
Tel: 020 7226 5879
Fax: 020 7354 8005

Women Prisoners Resource Centre

This is a national organisation. They offer advice to women ex-prisoners, including information on housing, benefits, training schemes and health.
1a Canalside House, 383 Ladbroke Grove, London, W10 5AA
Tel: 020 8968 3121

Prostitution

ANAWIM

Helps young women prostitutes.
166 Mary Street, Balsall Heath, Birmingham, B12 9RJ
Tel: 0121 440 5296

EXIT 2

This organisation helps young women who want to leave the sex industry.
PO Box 448, Bradford BD4 8YJ

Housing

Centrepoint

Houses young people at risk.
Central Office, Bewlay House, 2 Swallow Place, London, W1R 7AA
Tel: 020 7544 5000
Fax: 020 7544 5001

Shelterline

24-hour free national housing helpline.
Call free: 0800 800 4444

Legal Advice

The Children's Legal Centre

Free and confidential legal advice and information for children and young people.
Tel: 01206 873820

Justice for Women

Campaigning against discrimination in law. One of the main aims of this organisation is to help women who have been imprisoned for hurting or killing abusive partners or males. They have centres in West Yorkshire (Tel: 0113 262 0293), Manchester (Tel: 0161 860 4384) and London (Tel: 020 8340 3699).

Prison

HIBISCUS

A sister organisation of the Female Prisoners Welfare Project. Deals mostly with Jamaican and Nigerian women and offers pre-trial/pre-conviction aid and support. Helps female prisoners to maintain links with their families and children back home and finds missing family members.
15 Great St Thomas Apostle, Mansion House, London, EC4V 2BB
Tel: 020 7329 2384

NACRO
Women prisoners resource centre.
Head Office, 169 Clapham Road, London, SW9 0PU
Tel: 020 7582 6500
Fax: 020 7735 4666